ADORABLE KNITS
FOR TINY TOTS

The Craft Library

ADORABLE KNITS
FOR TINY TOTS

25 stylish designs from 6 months to 4 years

Zoë Mellor

hamlyn

This book is dedicated to Toby
and Kitty – great little inspirations
for my life and work.

An Hachette UK Company
www.hachette.co.uk

First published in Great Britain in 2004
by Hamlyn,
a division of Octopus Publishing Group Ltd
Endeavour House
189 Shaftesbury Avenue
London
WC2H 8JY
www.octopusbooks.co.uk

This edition published in 2011

This material was previously published as
Adorable Knits for Tiny Tots

ISBN 978-0-600-62382-3

A CIP catalogue record for this book is
available from the British Library.

Printed and bound in China

10 9 8 7 6 5 4 3 2 1

contents

introduction

As I am now the mother of two – Toby is four and Kitty is 11 months – I have really enjoyed designing the knits for this book. My children are a great inspiration to me and I always design with them in mind. Toby is modelling the pirate sweater – he loves the idea of being a pirate. The fairy dress is a favourite with Toby's girl friends for the many fancy dress parties in their toddler social calendar.

A busy mother myself, I know that if you are going to make the effort to knit, it has to be for a very special item and that the knitting process has to be relaxing. This is why I always use the best-quality yarns. They feel gorgeous to knit with and provide perfect comfort for those little ones with sensitive skin.

As well as sweaters, dresses and jackets, I have included hats, mittens and bootees in my tiny tots collection. The small accessories make great newborn presents and there are two simple baby blankets, sure to give many years of use. My personal favourites in this collection are the pinafore dress, the striped hat and scarf set, and the lacy sweater.

I hope you discover many favourites of your own here and have fun knitting them. And may the tiny tots in your life enjoy wearing your knits as much as mine do!

Happy knitting!

Zoë Mellor

yarns & colours

When creating knits for children it is important to give equal importance to the comfort of the yarns and to the allover look of the outfit. My own two children are always in my mind when I am designing and I stick to what would suit them. Children should keep their innocence for as long as possible and have fun in what they wear.

Designing for children has fewer restraints than designing for adults, as children seem happier to wear brighter shades and enjoy a sense of fun in their clothing. Be sure to take the opportunity to try out different colours from the ones I have used. You'll get a lot of satisfaction knitting up swatches while playing with colour schemes.

Colour has such a strong effect on a design – the same design can look so totally different made in a different set of shades. This is simply illustrated in the striped tank tops on page 52. Experiment with colours that catch your eye. Adding your own touches to designs will make you treasure them even more.

choosing yarn

It is a good idea to buy the yarn brand recommended in my knitting patterns. I will have chosen the yarn because its weight and texture perfectly suit that particular design. Since comfort is a top priority for kids' knits, cotton yarns feature prominently in my designs. They are soft enough for children's sensitive skin, aren't itchy and are ideal to wear all year round – warm in winter and cool in summer.

Consider the qualities of the yarn you're going to use before starting your tiny tot knit. Synthetics may be easy to wash, but natural fibres maintain their elegance for many years and get even better with age. Tiny tot knits in natural fibres can be passed down to a new sibling and still look good. Here are the pros of my favourite yarns – wool, cotton and cashmere:

wool is traditionally associated with knitting. It is springier than cotton and is warm and great for cold weather. Taking dyes well, it comes in masses of good colours. Some wool yarns, such as Botany, are softer to the touch than others, so pick them carefully.

cotton allows your skin to breathe. It is cooler than wool and non-itchy, making it ideal as an all-year-round yarn. As cotton is not as elastic as wool, maintain a fairly tight tension when knitting it up so that your knit holds its shape properly.

cotton-and-wool-mixed yarn is a great choice for children's knits. Combining the best qualities of both wool and cotton, it is warm, comfortable, non-itchy, washes well and holds its shape well.

cashmere is amazingly soft to the touch. Like wool it holds its shape well when knitted. Cashmere does have to be washed with care so it may be better used in items for special occasions. It is ideal for children with very sensitive skin.

yarn and dye lots

Yarn is dyed in batches and dye lots can vary greatly. It is essential to check the dye lot number on your yarn label to make sure that you use the same dye lot for the main colour of your knit, otherwise you run the risk of your garment being unintentionally stripy. If it is not possible to get all the yarn you need for your main colour from the same dye lot, use the odd ball for the ribbed borders. The raised texture of the ribbing disguises the colour discrepancy. For colours dotted around the design, variations in dye lots won't matter as long as they aren't touching each other.

substituting yarn

If you want to knit with different yarns from those specified in the patterns, please remember to think about the stitch size and the weight of the yarn. A yarn might knit up to the right number of stitches and rows to the centimetre (inch) but the resulting fabric may be so heavy that it pulls your design out of shape. Before you use a different yarn, I recommend that you knit a tension (gauge) square to check the stitch size and then see if you like the feel of the fabric.

colour knitting

Many of the patterns in this book involve colour knitting techniques. If the design is not a Fair Isle and the colours are in blocks, use the intarsia method of colour knitting. An example of intarsia knitting is the motif on the Pirate Sweater (see page 60). When working intarsia, do not carry the yarn across the back of the work; instead use a separate ball of yarn for each isolated area of colour. Where a block of colour is small, you can use a long length of yarn or a small amount wound around a bobbin. The intarsia method prevents the knitting from becoming too bulky and also avoids pulling and distortion across the motif. When changing from one colour to another, twist the yarns around each other to prevent holes from forming. If you still see holes at the colour-change

points, try twisting the yarn twice to pull the colours even closer together.

When knitting a Fair Isle design, strand the yarns across the back of the work, picking them up and dropping them as they are needed. Make sure that you don't pull the yarns too tightly, as this will distort the shape of the knitting and make the garment narrower than it should be. The back of the Fair Isle should not have very long loops, as this type of design is repetitive and the yarn colours repeat every few stitches. If the loops are too long they can get caught and pulled by tiny fingers.

the right size for tiny tots

Knitting patterns always give the finished knitted measurement of the garment around the chest, the garment length and the sleeve seam. A good way to check that you are choosing the right size is to match these measurements to a knit that you know is just right for your tiny tot. If in doubt, pick the next size up, as the child will soon grow into it.

Once you've chosen the right size in which to knit the pattern, all you need to do is make sure your knitting turns out the way it should. Tension (gauge) is probably the most important thing to get right when beginning to knit a pattern or even to design knitwear. Many knitters get so carried away with wanting to get knitting that they don't bother to knit a test square. Please do bother – it can make the difference between a professional-looking garment and a badly fitted garment.

Tension (gauge) is simply the measurement of the tightness or looseness of the knitted fabric. On most yarn labels the recommended tension (gauge) is given in terms of the number of stitches and the number of rows over 10cm (4in) of stocking (stockinette) stitch.

Tension (gauge) determines the measurements of the garment, so if the tension (gauge) you knit to does not match that shown in the pattern, your garment will end up the wrong size. Always work to the tension (gauge) provided in your knitting pattern – designers will have knit their own swatches, which

may be slightly different from the stitch size given on the yarn label. Use the needle size specified in the pattern as well, at least for your first attempt at a test swatch. Generally, the finer the yarn the smaller the needle size used for it, and the thicker the yarn the bigger the needles. I tend to use medium-weight yarns because I like to see my knitting grow quite quickly. Kids' knits are small garments anyway, so speedy results are guaranteed.

measuring tension (gauge)

To measure your tension (gauge), first knit a swatch at least 15cm (6in) square. This gives you plenty of room to accurately measure the number of stitches and rows over 10cm (4in); it can be hard to measure a smaller swatch accurately, since the edges curl up slightly. Flatten your swatch on a table top or pin it to your ironing board until it is flat. Steam press if necessary (see Blocking, page 15).

To check stitch tension (gauge), measure with a ruler and use pins to mark 10cm (4in) widthways across your swatch; always measure from the centre of your swatch. Count the number of stitches between the pins. To check row tension (gauge), do the same, but lengthways. If the number of stitches/ rows is greater than that quoted in the pattern, your stitch size is too small. This can be remedied by using larger needles than stated in the pattern. If the number of stitches/rows is fewer than that quoted in the pattern, your stitch size is too big and you need to use smaller needles than stated in the pattern. Keep doing test squares, changing needle size as required, until you get the right tension (gauge).

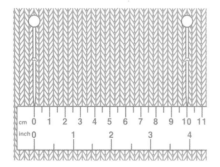

When you actually begin to knit your garment, you may find that with more stitches on the needles you are knitting more tightly or loosely. If you think this is happening, check your tension (gauge) on the actual garment, too, and adjust the needle size if necessary.

sizing up patterns

Knitters often ask me if I can give them instructions for the next size up of a design. This is not always a quick calculation to make and I am rarely able to supply such tailor-made patterns. However, as a general rule knitters can make these amendments to my patterns themselves without too much trouble. When designing, I usually use simple shapes and set-in square sleeves which are easy to size up.

altering the length

To change the length of a garment, you need to add more rows. The pattern tension (gauge) will tell you how many rows you need for 10cm (4in). Simply divide that number by 10 to find out how many extra rows will make 1cm (or divide that number by 4 to find out how many extra rows will make an extra inch). Measure the child you are making the garment for to see how much longer you need to make it. For example, if you need to make the design 2.5cm (1in) longer, just multiply your centimetre calculation by 2.5 (or multiply your inch calculation by 1).

altering the width

Change the width of a garment in the same way that you would change the length – use the number of stitches per 10cm (4in) to calculate how many stitches to add.

a simple reminder

When altering the lengths and widths of my knitting, I find it handy to start out by jotting down the following:
1cm (or inch) up = X rows
1cm (or inch) across = X stitches

Fill in the X's with your calculations and refer back to these notes whenever you need to.

finishing your garment

Finishing your garment well is essential for achieving a successful and professional-looking garment. Although the processes involved can be time consuming, it is time well spent, for careless finishing can spoil the effect of even the most beautiful knitting.

sewing in yarn ends

The number of yarn ends left when a garment is completed can be astonishing – and daunting. Many knitters I know find the first stage in finishing – sewing in yarn ends – a tedious task. They would rather start knitting their next project than finish the job in hand. Over the years I have grown fonder of sewing in ends; it can be quite therapeutic! A quick way I have discovered is first to weave a darning needle through the back of the knitting and then thread the end through. This prevents short ends from slipping out of the needle as you weave.

mattress stitch

Sewing perfect seams is very important. Mattress stitch is the most basic seaming technique. I use it probably more than any other method as it produces a totally invisible and straight seam. It is especially useful when seaming a striped garment. If backstitch is used, which entails pinning the pieces together with right sides facing, stripes can move out of alignment, whereas mattress stitch, which avoids pinning and is worked on the right side, will achieve a perfect match.

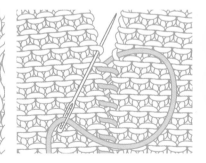

1 With the right sides facing you, insert your blunt-ended sewing needle into the knitting between the first and second stitches on the first row of the seam.

2 Then insert the needle in the other piece, in the centre of the second stitch in from the edge. Link the sides in a zigzag manner as shown above.

3 On garter stitch, work through the lower loop on one edge, then through the upper loop of the corresponding stitch on the other edge.

backstitch

Backstitch is good for sewing in sleeves or for tidying edges with lots of colour joins.

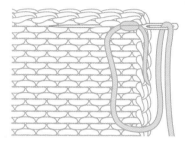 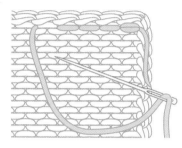

1 With right sides together, secure the seam with a starting stitch. Bring the sewing needle through both pieces of knitting, making your first stitch about 1cm (⅜in) in size.

2 Then loop back to where the yarn came out of your stitch and bring the needle out a little past the end of the last stitch. Continue like this, taking the needle backward and forward with each stitch.

blocking

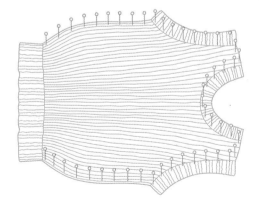

Blocking, or pressing, your pieces of knitting before sewing the seams gives a more professional finish, as the edges will be flatter and not curl up. Always check the yarn label for temperatures and to see if you can press directly onto your knitting. Most of the yarns I have chosen can be pressed, but if your yarn contains acrylic it may not be suitable for pressing.

To block your knitting, carefully pin each piece face down on a flat surface – I find the ironing board ideal. While pinning the pieces, gently nudge them into the desired shape without pulling the stitches too tightly. Then lightly press or steam the knitted fabric (on the back of the work) until it is flat. If you steam your knitting, remember to let it dry out completely before removing the pins.

edgings and buttons

The simpler the shape and design of the garment the more perfect your finishing touches have to be. I love simple contrasting edges that give the garment that little special detail. Even simply casting on or casting (binding) off with a contrasting colour can create a surprisingly effective border. It can also highlight the motif or another element of the design. Contrasting edges feature on the Strawberries & Cream Sweater on page 64, the Heart-motif Cardigan on page 70 and the Ship-ahoy! Sweater on page 82.

Once your knitted garment is blocked and stitched together, you are ready to sew on the buttons if there are any. Choose interesting buttons for the perfect personal touch, but try not to let them take your design over – sometimes 'less is more'. Usually, the simpler the design the more detailed the buttons can be, and the more complicated the knitted fabric the simpler the buttons should be. Take your finished knitting with you when buying your buttons so you can test the effect different buttons have on the garment.

cotton candy

daisy dress

This simple flower-motif dress is really beautiful. Knitted in cotton, it is cool and comfortable and great for those hot summer days.

materials

3(4:4:5) 50g/1¾oz balls of Jaeger *Siena* in main colour **M** (turquoise/Borage 424 or mauve/Lavender 404) and one ball each in **A** (hot pink/Petunia 423) and **B** (red/Chilli 425 or white/White 401)

Pair each of 2¾mm(US 2) and 3mm(US 3) knitting needles

sizes

to fit				
6–12 mths	1–2	2–3	3–4	yrs
actual measurements				
chest (underarm)				
53	58	62	68	cm
20¼	22¾	24½	26¼	in
length to shoulder				
37	43	45	47	cm
14½	17	17¾	18½	in

tension/gauge

29 sts and 38 rows to 10cm/4in over st-st using 3mm(US 3) needles

abbreviations

alt alternate; **beg** beginning; **cm** centimetre(s): **cont** continu(e)(ing); **dec** decrease; **foll** follow(s)(ing); **in** inch(es); **k** knit; **p** purl; **rem** remaining; **rep** repeat; **RS** right side; **sl** slip; **ssk** sl 1 knitwise, sl 1 knitwise, insert tip of left needle into fronts of 2 slipped sts and k2tog tbl; **st(s)** stitch(es); **st-st** stocking/stockinette stitch; **tbl** through back of loop(s); **tog** together; **WS** wrong side

back

With 2¾mm(US 2) needles and A, cast on
119(123:129:135) sts.

Work 3cm/1¼in in garter st (knit every row).

Change to 3mm(US 3) needles and M.

Beg with a RS (k) row, work 4 rows in st-st, so ending
with a WS (p) row.

Next row (RS) K3, ssk, k to last 5 sts, k2tog, k3.

Cont in st-st, work 3(3:5:5) rows.

Rep last 4(4:6:6) rows 20(18:18:17) times more.
77(85:91:99) sts.

Cont straight until work measures
28(34:35:37)cm/11(13¼:13¼:14½)in from cast-on edge,
ending with a WS row.

Shape armholes

Cast/bind off 5(6:6:6) sts at beg of next 2 rows.
67(73:79:87) sts.

Next row (RS) K1, ssk, k to last 3 sts, k2tog, k1.

Next row (WS) P1, p2tog, p to last 3 sts, p2tog tbl, p1.

Rep last 2 rows 2(3:3:4) times more. 55(57:63:67) sts.

Cont straight for 24(22:26:24) rows, so ending with a WS
row.

shape back neck

Next row (RS) K19(20:21:23) sts, turn and cont on
these sts only, leaving rem sts on a spare needle.

**Cast/bind off 3 sts at beg (neck edge) of next row and
2 sts at beg of foll alt row.

Work 1 row.

Dec 1 st at beg of next row.

Cast/bind off rem 13(14:15:17) sts.

With RS facing, slip 17(17:21:21) sts at centre back onto a
holder, rejoin yarn to rem sts and k to end. Work 1 row.

Complete to match first side from **.

front

Work as for Back until Front measures
20(26:27:29)cm/7¾(10:10½:11¼)in from cast-on edge,
ending with a WS row.

Place first row of chart centrally on next row and work all
27 rows in st-st from chart **and at the same time** cont

to shape sides as for Back.

When chart and side shaping have been worked, cont straight in st-st until front matches Back to armhole, ending with a WS row.

Shape armholes

Cast/bind off 5(6:6:6) sts at beg of next 2 rows. 67(73:79:87) sts.

Next row (RS) K1, ssk, k to last 3 sts, k2tog, k1.

Next row (WS) P1, p2tog, p to last 3 sts, p2tog tbl, p1.

Rep last 2 rows 2(3:3:4) times more, so ending with a WS row. 55(57:63:67) sts.

Shape front neck

Next row (RS) K22(23:25:27) sts, turn and cont on these sts only, leaving rem sts on a spare needle.

**Cast/bind off 2 sts at beg (neck edge) of next and foll alt row, then dec 1 st at beg of foll 5(5:6:6) alt rows. 13(14:15:17) sts.

Cont straight for 16(14:16:14) rows more.

Cast/bind off.

With RS facing, slip 11(11:13:13) sts at centre front onto a holder, rejoin yarn to rem sts and k to end. Work 1 row.

Complete to match first side from **.

neck edging

Join right shoulder.

With RS facing, 2¼mm(US 2) needles and A, pick up and k 32(32:34:34) sts down left front neck, k across 11(11:13:13) sts at centre front, pick up and k 32(32:34:34) sts up right front neck, 9 sts down right back neck, k across 17(17:21:21) sts at centre back, then pick up and k 9 sts up left back neck. 110(110:120:120) sts.

K 2 rows.

Cast/bind off knitwise.

armhole edging

Join left shoulder and neck edge seam.

With RS facing, 2¼mm(US 2) needles and A, pick up and k 82(82:92:92) sts around armhole edge.

K 2 rows.

Cast/bind off knitwise.

to finish

Join side and armhole edge seams.

flower chart

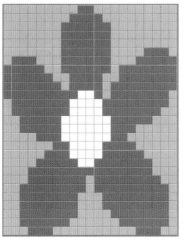

key

■	A
■	M
□	B

little star sweater

Green and turquoise is a great colour combination for both girls and boys. The 'little star' in your life will love the striped arms and star on this sweater.

materials

3(3:4:4) 50g/1¾oz balls of Rowan *Cotton Glacé* in main colour **M** (turquoise/Pier 809) and one ball each in **A** (light green/Bud 800) and **B** (off-white/Ecru 725)

Pair of 3¾mm(US 5) knitting needles

sizes

to fit				
6–12 mths	1–2	2–3	3–4	yrs
actual measurements				
chest				
56	61	66	71	cm
22	24	26	28	in
length				
30	33	36	38	cm
11¾	13	14	15	in
sleeve seam				
18	21	23	28	cm
7	8¼	9	11	in

tension/gauge

23 sts and 32 rows to 10cm/4in over st-st using 3¾mm(US 5) needles

abbreviations

alt alternate; **beg** beginning; **cm** centimetre(s); **cont** continu(e)(ing); **dec** decrease; **foll** follow(s)(ing); **in** inch(es); **inc** increase; **k** knit; **p** purl; **patt** pattern; **rem** remaining **rep** repeat **RS** right side; **st(s)** stitch(es) **st-st** stocking/ stockinette stitch; **WS** wrong side

note

When working from chart, use a separate small ball of yarn for motif, twisting yarns at colour change to avoid holes.

back

With 3¾mm(US 5) needles and M, cast on 64(70:76:82) sts.

Beg with a RS (k) row, work 5 rows in st-st.

Change to A and p 1 row.

Now work in rib as foll:

1st rib row (RS) K1(2:1:2), p2, [k2, p2] to last 1(2:1:2) sts, k1(2:1:2).

2nd rib row (WS) P1(2:1:2), k2, [p2, k2] to last 1(2:1:2) sts, p1(2:1:2).

Rep last 2 rows 4 times more.**

Change to M.

Beg with a RS (K) row, work 48(54:60:64) rows in st-st.

shape armholes

Cont in st-st, cast/bind off 5(5:6:6) sts at beg of next 2 rows.

Cont straight for 36(40:42:46) rows more.

star chart

key
- ☐ B
- ☐ M

shape shoulders

Cast/bind off 8(9:9:10) sts at beg of next 2 rows and 7(8:9:10) sts at beg of foll 2 rows.

Leave rem 24(26:28:30) sts on a holder.

front

Work as for Back to **.

Change to M.

Beg with a RS (K) row, work 18(22:26:28) rows in st-st, so ending with a WS (p) row.

place motif

Next row (RS) K12(15:18:21)M, k across 40 sts of first row of chart, k12(15:18:21)M.

Cont in st-st foll chart until chart row 30(32:34:36) has been worked.

shape armholes

Keeping chart correct, cast/bind off 5(5:6:6) sts at beg of next 2 rows.

Cont straight until all 50 chart rows have been worked.

Work 4(8:12:16) rows more, so ending with a WS row.

shape neck

Next row (RS) K22(25:27:30), turn and cont on these sts only, leaving rem sts on a spare needle.

Cast/bind off 2 sts at beg (neck edge) of next and foll alt row, then dec 1 st at beg of next 3(4:5:6) alt rows.

Work 4(4:2:2) rows more.

shape shoulder

Cast/bind off 8(9:9:10) sts at beg of next row and rem 7(8:9:10) sts at beg of foll alt row.

With RS facing, slip 10 sts at centre front onto a holder, rejoin yarn to rem sts and complete to match first side, reversing shaping.

sleeves

With 3¾mm(US 5) needles and M, cast on 36(38:38:40) sts.

Beg with a RS (k) row, work 5 rows in st-st.

Change to A and p 1 row.

Now work in rib as foll:

1st rib row (RS) K1(2:2:1), p2, [k2, p2] to last

1(2:2:1) sts, k1(2:2:1).

2nd rib row (WS) P1(2:2:1), k2, [p2, k2] to last 1(2:2:1) sts, p1(2:2:1).

Rep last 2 rows 4 times more.

Change to M.

Beg with a RS (k) row, work alternating 10-row st-st stripes of M and C **and at the same time** inc 1 st at each end of 3rd(3rd:5th:5th) row and every foll 4th row until there are 60(64:68:72) sts.

Cont straight until sleeve measures 15(18:20:25)cm/6(7:7¾:9¾)in from end of ribbing.

Mark each end of last row, then work 6(6:8:8) rows more.

Cast/bind off.

neckband

Join right shoulder seam.

With RS facing, 3¼mm (US 5) needles and A, pick up and k 17(19:19:21) sts down left front neck, k across 10(10:12:12) sts at centre front, pick up and k 17(19:19:21) sts up right front neck, then k across 24(26:28:30) sts at centre back. 68(74:78:84) sts.

1st rib row (WS) P1(2:2:1), k2, [p2, k2] to last 1(2:2:1) sts, p1(2:2:1).

2nd rib row (RS) K1(2:2:1), p2, [k2, p2] to last 1(2:2:1) sts, k1(2:2:1).

Rep last 2 rows twice more and first rib row again.

Change to M and work 6 rows in st-st, beg with a RS (k) row.

Cast/bind off.

to finish

Join left shoulder and neckband seam. Sew sleeves into armholes, joining row ends above markers to cast-/bound-off sts at underarm. Join side and sleeve seams.

lacy sweater

Pretty without being fussy or frilly, this sweater's lacy edging picks up on the flower motif. It looks great worn with simple linen trousers.

materials

6(6:7:7) 50g/1¾oz balls of Rowan *Handknit DK Cotton* in pink/Sugar 303

Pair each of 3¾mm(US 5) and 4mm(US 6) knitting needles

sizes

to fit

6–12 mths	1–2	2–3	3–4	yrs
actual measurements				
chest				
56	61	66	71	cm
22	24	26	28	in
length				
33	36	39	41	cm
13	14	15¼	16¼	in
sleeve seam				
18	21	23	27	cm
7	8¼	9	10½	in

tension/gauge

20 sts and 28 rows to 10cm/4in over reverse st-st using 4mm(US 6) needles

abbreviations

alt alternate; **beg** beginning; **cm** centimetre(s); **cont** continu(e)(ing); **dec** decrease; **foll** follow(s)(ing); **in** inch(es); **inc** increase; **k** knit; **kfb** k into front and back of next st; **MB (make bobble)** [k1, p1, k1, p1, k1] into next st, turn, p5, turn, pass 2nd, 3rd, 4th and 5th sts over first st and k this st tbl; **p** purl; **patt** pattern; **pfb** p into front and back of next st; **psso** pass slipped st over; **rem** remaining; **rep** repeat; **RS** right side; **skpo** sl 1, k1, pass slipped st over; **sl** slip; **st(s)** stitch(es); **st-st** stocking/stockinette stitch; **tbl** through back of loops; **tog** together; **WS** wrong side; **yf (yarn forward)** bring yarn forward between needles and over right needle to make a st; **yo (yarn over needle)** take yarn over right needle to make a st; **yrn (yarn round needle)** wrap yarn around right needle from front to back and bring to front again between needles to make a st; **ytf (yarn to front)** bring yarn to front of work

stitch patterns

diagonal edging

Worked over 8 sts.

1st foundation row (RS) K6, kfb, ytf, sl 1 purlwise. 9 sts.

2nd foundation row (WS) K1tbl, k1, [yf, skpo, k1] twice, ytf, sl 1 purlwise. 9 sts.

1st row K1tbl, k to last st, kfb, turn and cast on 2 sts. 12 sts.

2nd row K1, kfb, k2, [yf, skpo, k1] twice, yf, k1, ytf, sl 1 purlwise. 14 sts.

3rd row K1tbl, k to last 2 sts, kfb, ytf, sl 1 purlwise. 15 sts.

4th row K1tbl, kfb, k2, [yf, skpo, k1] 3 times, k1, ytf, sl 1 purlwise. 16 sts.

5th row K1tbl, k to last 2 sts, k2tog. 15 sts.

6th row Sl 1 purlwise, k1, psso, skpo, k4, [yf, skpo, k1] twice, ytf, sl 1 purlwise. 13 sts.

7th row K1 tbl, k to last 2 sts, k2tog. 12 sts.

8th row Cast/bind off 3 sts, k2, yf, skpo, k1, yf, skpo, ytf, sl 1 purlwise. 9 sts.

The last 8 rows form the patt and are repeated.

flower motif

Worked on a background of reverse st-st over 15 sts.

1st row (RS) P5, k2, p1, k2, p5.

2nd row K5, p2, k1, p2, k5.

3rd row P4, k2tog, k1, yrn, p1, yo, k1, skpo, p4.

4th row K4, p3, k1, p3, k4.

5th row P3, k2tog, k1, yf, k1, p1, k1, yf, k1, skpo, p3.

6th row K3, p4, k1, p4, k3.

7th row P2, k2tog, k1, yf, k2, p1, k2, yf, k1, skpo, p2.

8th row K2, p5, k1, p5, k2.

9th row P1, k2tog, k1, yf, k3, p1, k3, yf, k1, skpo, p1.

10th row K1, [p6, k1] twice.

11th row [K2tog, k1, yf, k1] twice, yf, k1, skpo, k1, yf, k1, skpo.

12th row P6, k1, p1, k1, p6.

13th row K3, k2tog, k1, yrn, p1, k1, p1, yo, k1, skpo, k3.

14th row P5, k2, p1, k2, p5.

15th row K2, k2tog, k1, yrn, p2, k1, p2, yo, k1, skpo, k2.

16th row P4, k3, p1, k3, p4.

17th row K1, k2tog, k1, yrn, p3, k1, p3, yo, k1, skpo, k1.

18th row P3, k4, p1, k4, p3.

19th row K2tog, k1, yrn, p3, MB, p1, MB, p3, yo, k1, skpo.

20th row P1, k13, p1.

21st row P4, MB, p5, MB, p4.

22nd, 24th, 26th, 28th and 30th rows K15.

23rd row P3, MB, p1, [p2tog, yrn] twice, p2, MB, p3.

25th row P3, MB, [p2tog, yrn] 3 times, p1, MB, p3.

27th row P3, MB, p1, [p2tog, yrn] twice, p2, MB, p3.

29th row P4, MB, p5, MB, p4.

31st row P6, MB, p1, MB, p6.

These 31 rows form the flower motif.

sleeve pattern stitch

1st and 2nd rows K.

3rd row (WS) P1, [yrn, p2tog] to end.

4th–6th rows K.

7th–10th rows Beg with a WS (p) row, work 4 rows in st-st.

These 10 rows form the patt and are repeated.

back

With 4mm(US 6) needles, cast on 8 sts.

Work 2 foundation rows of diagonal edging, then work 8-row rep of edging 14(16:18:19) times, ending with an 8th row.
Cast/bind off.

With RS facing, pick up and k55(65:71:73) sts along unscalloped edge of edging.

1st row (WS) P1, pfb, p to last 3 sts, pfb, p2. 57(67:73:75) sts.

K 3 rows.

5th row (WS) P1, [yrn, p2tog] to end.

K 3 rows.**

Beg with a WS (k) row, work in reverse st-st for 27(33:41:45) rows.

shape armholes

Cont in reverse st-st, cast/bind off 3(3:4:4) sts at beg of next 2 rows. 51(61:65:67) sts.

Work 28(30:32:34) rows more in reverse st-st.

shape back neck and shoulders

Next row (RS) P18(20:21:22), turn and cont on these sts only, leaving rem sts on a spare needle.

Cast/bind off 2 sts at beg (neck edge) of next and foll alt row.
Cast/bind off rem 14(16:17:18) sts.
With RS facing, slip 15(21:23:23) sts at centre back onto a holder, rejoin yarn to rem sts and p to end.
K 1 row.
Cast/bind off 2 sts at beg (neck edge) of next and foll alt row.
Cast/bind off rem 14(16:17:18) sts.

front

Work as for Back to **.
Beg with a WS (k) row, work in reverse st-st for 15(21:31:37) rows.
place flower motif
Next row (RS) P21(26:29:30), work 15 sts of first row of flower motif, p21(26:29:30).
Next row K21(26:29:30), work 2nd row of flower motif, k21(26:29:30).
These 2 rows set position of motif.
Work 10(10:8:6) rows more as set.
shape armhole
Cont to work motif in position as set, cast/bind off 3(3:4:4) sts at beg of next 2 rows. 51(61:65:67) sts.
Work rem 17(17:19:21) motif rows.
Cont in reverse st-st, work 1(3:3:3) rows more, so ending with a WS row.
shape neck
Next row (RS) P20(24:25:26), turn and cont on these sts only, leaving rem sts on a spare needle.
***Cast/bind off 2(3:3:3) sts at beg (neck edge) of next row, 2 sts at beg of foll 1(2:2:2) alt rows and 1 st at beg of next 2(1:1:1) alt rows. Work 6 rows.
Cast/bind off rem 14(16:17:18) sts.
With RS facing, slip 11(13:15:15) sts at centre front onto a holder, rejoin yarn to rem sts on spare needle and p to end.
K 1 row.
Complete to match first side from *** to end.

sleeves

With 4mm(US 6) needles, cast on 33(33:35:35) sts.
Work in sleeve patt st, inc 1 st at each end of every 6th and foll 4th rows alternately until there are 51(53:57:59) sts, taking all inc sts into patt.
Cont straight in patt until sleeve measures 18(21:23:27)cm/7(8¼:9:10½)in from cast-on edge.
Mark each end of last row, then work 4(4:5:5) rows more.
Cast/bind off.

neckband

Join right shoulder seam.
With RS facing and 3¾mm(US 5) needles, pick up and k 17(17:18:18) sts down left front neck, k across 11(13:15:15) sts at centre front, pick up and k 18(18:19:19) sts up right front neck and 6 sts down right back neck, k across 15(21:23:23) sts at centre back and inc 2 sts evenly for first size only, then pick up and k 6 sts up left back neck. 75(81:87:87) sts.
1st and 2nd rows K.
3rd row (WS) P1, [yrn, p2tog] to end.
4th–6th rows K.
Cast/bind off knitwise.

to finish

Join left shoulder and neckband seam. Sew sleeves into armholes, joining row ends above markers to cast-/bound-off sts at underarm. Join sleeve, side and edging seams.

little blossom cardigan

This cardigan is guaranteed to catch everyone's eye with its scattered flowers. Its classic design means that it can be worn every day or dressed up for special occasions.

materials

4(4:5:6) 50g/1¾oz balls of Jaeger *Aqua* in main colour **M** (hot pink/ India 322), 2(2:3:3) balls in **A** (off-white/Creme 301) and one ball in **B** (pastel pink/Anemone 327)

Pair each of 3¼mm(US 3) and 3¾mm(US 5) knitting needles

5(5:6:6) buttons

sizes

to fit

6–12 mths	1–2	2–3	3–4	yrs
actual measurements				
chest				
56	61	66	71	cm
22	24	26	28	in
length				
30	33	36	38	cm
11¼	13	14	15	in
sleeve seam				
18	21	23	27	cm
7	8¼	9	10½	in

tension/gauge

22 sts and 30 rows to 10cm/4in over st-st using 3¾mm(US 5) needles

abbreviations

beg beginning; **cm** centimetre(s); **cont** continu(e)(ing); **dec** decrease; **foll** follow(s)(ing); **in** inch(es); **inc** increase; **k** knit; **p** purl; **patt** pattern; **rem** remaining; **rep** repeat; **RS** right side; **st(s)** stitch(es); **st-st** stocking/stockinette stitch; **tog** together; **WS** wrong side; **yrn (yarn round needle)** bring yarn to front between needles, then wrap yarn around right needle from front to back and bring it to front again between needles to make a st

note

When working from chart, work in st-st and use separate length of yarn for each motif, twisting yarns at colour change to avoid holes.

back

With 3¼mm(US 3) needles and M, cast on 61(67:73:79) sts.

Moss/seed st row K1, [p1, k1] to end.

Rep last row 4 times more.

Change to 3¾mm(US 5) needles.

Next row (RS) Moss/seed st 5, k51(57:63:69) from chart, moss/seed st 5.

Next row (WS) Moss/seed st 5, p51(57:63:69) from chart, moss/seed st 5.

These last 2 rows set the position of the st-st with moss/seed st side-slit sts.

Rep last 2 rows 3(3:5:5) times more.

Now work from chart in st-st only until chart row 50(56:62:68) has been worked, so ending with a WS row.

shape armholes

Cont from chart, cast/bind off 5(5:6:6) sts at beg of next 2 rows.

Cont straight on rem 51(57:61:67) sts until chart row 84(92:100:108) has been worked, so ending with a WS row.

shape shoulders

Cast/bind off 15(17:19:21) sts at beg of next 2 rows.

Leave rem 21(23:23:25) sts on a holder.

pocket linings (make 2)

With 3¼mm(US 5) needles and M, cast on 17(19:19:21) sts.

Beg with a RS (k) row, work 20(20:22:22) rows in st-st.

Leave sts on a holder.

left front

With 3¼mm(US 3) needles and M, cast on 34(37:40:43) sts.

Work 5 rows in moss/seed st as for Back.

Change to 3¾mm(US 5) needles and work in st-st from chart between lines for correct size and garment piece, keeping 5 sts in moss/seed st in M at beg and end of first 8(8:12:12) rows and then at end of every RS row and beg of every WS row for button band. Work until 24(24:26:26) chart rows have been worked, so ending with a WS row.

place pocket

Next row (RS) K6(7:10:11) sts in patt, slip next 17(19:19:21) sts onto a holder, k in patt across 17(19:19:21) sts of first pocket lining, k6 in patt, moss/seed st 5 in M.

Cont to work in patt until chart row 50(56:62:68) has been worked, so ending with a WS row.

shape armhole

Cont in patt, cast/bind off 5(5:6:6) sts at beg of next row.

Cont straight on rem 29(32:34:37) sts until chart row 68(76:84:92) has been worked, so ending with a WS row.

shape neck

Next row (RS) Patt to last 5 sts and slip these rem 5 moss/seed sts at front edge onto a safety pin for neckband.

Cast/bind off 3 sts at beg of next row.

Dec 1 st at neck edge on foll 6(7:7:8) rows.

Cont straight in patt until chart row 84(92:100:108) has been worked.

Cast/bind off rem 15(17:19:21) sts for shoulder.

Mark the position for 5(5:6:6) buttons on the button band, the first on the 5th row of lower moss/seed st band, the last just below the neck edge and the rem 3(3:4:4) spaced evenly between.

front, back
and sleeve
chart

key

■ M
■ B
□ A

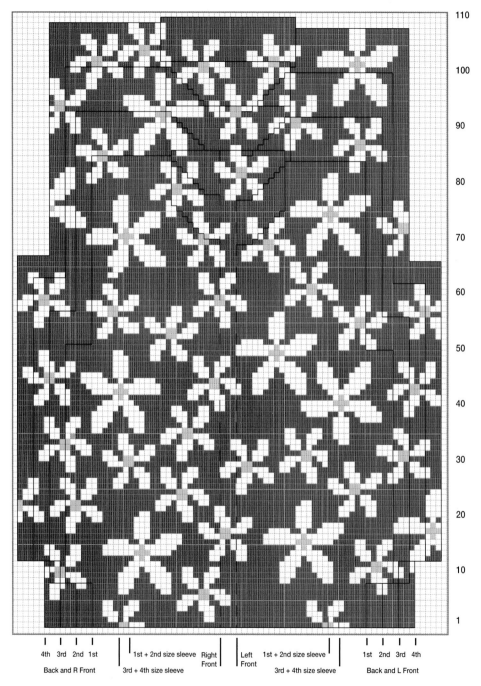

110

100

90

80

70

60

50

40

30

20

10

1

4th   3rd 2nd 1st   1st + 2nd size sleeve   Right   Left   1st + 2nd size sleeve   1st   2nd 3rd 4th
                                                    Front   Front
Back and R Front   3rd + 4th size sleeve   3rd + 4th size sleeve   Back and L Front

right front

With 3¼mm(US 3) needles and M, cast on 34(37:40:43) sts.

Work 4 rows in moss/seed st as for Back.

Work first buttonhole on next row to match position of first button as foll:

Buttonhole row (RS) K1, p2tog, yrn, p1, k1, patt to end.

Change to 3¼mm(US 5) needles and work in st-st from chart between lines for correct size and garment piece, keeping 5 sts in moss/seed st in M at beg and end of first 8(8:12:12) rows of chart and then at beg of every RS row and end of every WS row for buttonhole band.

Cont to work buttonholes as before to match markers throughout, work until 24(24:26:26) chart rows have been worked, so ending with a WS row.

place pocket

Next row (RS) Moss/seed st 5 in M, k6 in patt, slip next 17(19:19:21) sts onto a holder, k in patt across 17(19:19:21) sts of second pocket lining, patt to end.

Cont to work in patt until chart row 51(57:63:69) has been worked, so ending with a RS row.

shape armhole

Cont in patt, cast/bind off 5(5:6:6) sts at beg of next row.

Cont straight on rem 29(32:34:37) sts until chart row 69(77:85:93) has been worked, so ending with a RS row.

shape neck

Next row (WS) Patt to last 5 sts and slip these rem 5 moss/seed sts at front edge onto a safety pin for neckband.

Cast/bind off 3 sts at beg of next row.

Dec 1 st at neck edge on foll 6(7:7:8) rows.

Cont straight in patt until chart row 85(93:101:109) has been worked.

Cast/bind off rem 15(17:19:21) sts for shoulder.

sleeves

With 3¼mm(US 3) needles and M, cast on 37(37:41:41) sts and work 5 rows in moss/seed st as for Back. Change to 3¼mm(US 5) needles.

Beg with a RS (k) row and working in st-st from chart, inc 1 st at each end of 5th and every foll 6th row until there are 51(53:55:57) sts, taking all inc sts into patt.

Cont straight until sleeve measures 18(21:23:27)cm/ 7(8¼:9:10½)in from cast-on edge.

Mark each end of last row, then work 6(6:7:7) rows more.

Cast/bind off in patt.

collar

Join shoulder seams.

With WS facing, 3¼mm(US 3) needles and M, moss/seed st 5 sts from safety pin of right front, turn and cast/bind off 3 sts, moss/seed st rem st on left needle, pick up and k 17 sts up Right Front neck, k across 21(23:23:25) sts at back neck, pick up and k 17 sts down left front neck and moss/seed st 5 from safety pin.

Next row Cast/bind off 3 sts, moss/seed st to end. 59(61:61:63) sts.

Work 2cm/¾in in moss/seed st.

Change to 3¼mm(US 5) needles and work 5cm/2in more in moss/seed st.

Cast/bind off in moss/seed st.

pocket top

With RS facing, 3¼mm(US 3) needles and M, k across 17(19:19:21) sts of pocket holder.

Work 4 rows in moss/seed st.

Cast/bind off.

to finish

Sew sleeves into armholes, joining row ends above markers to cast-/bound-off sts at underarm. Join sleeve seams. Join side seams above moss/seed st side slits. Sew pocket lining and pocket top edges in place. Sew on buttons.

fair isle cardigan

The subtle colours in this design create a modern twist on the classic Fair Isle cardigan. The little collar and mother-of-pearl buttons give it a simple, uncluttered finish.

materials

1(2:2:2) 50g/1¾oz balls of Rowan *Cotton Glacé*
in main colour **M** (purple/Hyacinth 787),
1(1:2:2) balls in **A** (rose pink/Bubbles 724)
and one ball each in **B** (lilac/Tickle 811), **C**
(light pink/Candy Floss 747), **D** (light
green/Bud 800), **E** (turquoise/Pier 809)
and **F** (off-white/Ecru 725)
Pair each of 3mm(US 2) and 3¼mm(US 3)
knitting needles
5(5:6:6) buttons

sizes

to fit				
6–12 mths	1–2	2–3	3–4	yrs
actual measurements				
chest				
56	61	66	71	cm
22	24	26	28	in
length				
30	33	36	38	cm
11¼	13	14	15	in
sleeve seam				
18	21	23	27	cm
7	8¼	9	10½	in

tension/gauge

26 sts and 31 rows to 10cm/4in over patterned
st-st using 3¼mm(US 3) needles

abbreviations

alt alternate; **beg** beginning; **cm** centimetre(s);
cont continu(e)(ing); **dec** decrease; **foll**
follow(s)(ing); **in** inch(es); **inc** increas(e)(ing);
k knit; **p** purl; **patt** pattern; **rem** remaining;
rep repeat; **RS** right side; **st(s)** stitch(es); **st-st**
stocking/stockinette stitch; **tbl** through back of
loop(s); **tog** together; **WS** wrong side

note

When working from chart, strand yarn not in use across
WS of work, weaving into back of sts where stranded
yarn crosses more than 5 sts.

back

With 3mm(US 2) needles and M, cast on 73(79:85:93) sts.

Moss/seed st row K1, [p1, k1] to end.

Rep last row 5 times more.

Change to 3¼mm(US 3) needles.

Beg with a RS (k) row, work in st-st from chart, placing marked st centrally.

Cont straight until back measures 19(21:23:24)cm/ 7½(8¼:9:9½)in from cast-on edge, ending with a WS row.

shape armholes

Cont from chart, cast/bind off 5(5:6:6) sts at beg of next 2 rows.

Cont straight on rem 63(69:73:81) sts until back measures 30(33:36:38)cm/11¾(13:14:15)in from cast-on edge, ending with a WS row.

shape shoulders

Cast/bind off 19(21:22:25) sts at beg of next 2 rows.

Leave rem 25(27:29:31) sts on a holder.

pocket lining (make 1)

With 3¼mm(US 3) needles and B (lilac), cast on 19(21:23:25) sts.

Beg with a RS (k) row, work 20(20:22:22) rows in st-st.

Leave sts on a holder.

left front

With 3mm(US 2) needles and M, cast on 39(41:45:49) sts.

Work 6 rows in moss/seed st as for Back, but inc 1 st at end of last row for 2nd size only. 39(42:45:49) sts.

Change to 3¼mm(US 3) needles and work in st-st from chart beg with same st as Back (3rd st to left of centre marked st for Right Front), keeping 5 sts in moss/seed st at end of every RS row and beg of every WS row for button band. Work until 22(22:24:24) chart rows have been worked, so ending with a WS row.

place pocket

Next row (RS) K9(10:11:13) sts in patt, slip next 19(21:23:25) sts onto a holder, k in patt across 19(21:23:25) sts of pocket lining, k6 in patt, moss/seed st 5 in M.

Cont to work in patt until front measures 19(21:23:24)cm/ 7½2(8¼:9:9½)in from cast-on edge, ending with a WS row (RS row for right front).

shape armhole

Cont in patt, cast/bind off 5(5:6:6) sts at beg of next row.

Cont straight on rem 34(37:39:43) sts until front measures 25(28:30:32)cm/10(11:11¾:12½)in from cast-on edge, ending with a RS row (WS row for right front).

shape neck

Cast/bind off 3 sts at beg of next row.

Next row Patt to last 2 sts and slip these last 2 sts at front edge onto a safety pin for collar.

Keeping chart patt correct, cast/bind off 3 sts at beg (neck edge) of next and foll alt row, then dec 1 st at neck edge on foll 4(5:6:7) alt rows.

Cont until front matches Back to shoulder.

shape shoulder

Cast/bind off rem 19(21:22:25) sts.

Mark the position for 5(5:6:6) buttons on the button band, the first on the 5th row of lower moss/seed st band, the last just below the neck edge with the rem 3(3:4:4) spaced evenly between.

right front

Work as for Left Front, but omitting pocket, working 5

moss/seed sts for buttonhole band at beg of RS rows and end of WS rows and noting bracketed exceptions (so reversing all shaping) **and at the same time** work buttonholes to match markers on Left Front when reached as foll:

1st buttonhole row (RS) K1, p2tog, make 2 *yarn overs* by wrapping yarn around right-hand needle from front to back and to front again and then over right-hand needle again ready to work next st, k2tog, patt to end.
2nd buttonhole row (WS) Work in patt, working [p1, k1tbl] into double yarn over of previous row.

sleeves

With 3mm(US 2) needles and M, cast on 35(37:39:41) sts and work 6 rows in moss/seed st as for Back.
Change to 3¼mm(US 3) needles.
Beg with a RS (k) row and working in st-st from chart, inc 1 st at each end of 5th and every foll 4th row until there are 57(63:67:73) sts, taking all inc sts into patt.
Cont straight until sleeve measures 18(21:23:27)cm/ 7(8¼:9:10½)in from cast-on edge.
Mark each end of last row, then work 6(6:7:7) rows more.
Cast/bind off in patt.

collar

Join shoulder seams.
With WS facing, 3mm(US 2) needles and M, moss/seed st 2 sts from safety pin on Right Front, turn and moss/seed st 2, pick up and k 13(13:15:15) sts up right front neck, k across 25(27:29:31) sts at back neck, pick up and k 13(13:15:15) sts down left front neck and moss/seed st 2 from safety pin. 55(57:63:65) sts.
Work 2cm/¾in in moss/seed st.
Change to 3¼mm(US 3) needles and work a further 4cm/1½in in moss/seed st.
Cast/bind off.

pocket top

With RS facing, 3mm(US 2) needles and M, k across 19(21:23:25) sts of pocket holder.

Work 4 rows in moss/seed st.
Cast/bind off.

to finish

Sew sleeves into armholes, joining row ends above markers to cast-/bound-off sts at underarm. Join side and sleeve seams. Sew pocket lining and pocket top edges in place. Sew on buttons.

fair isle chart

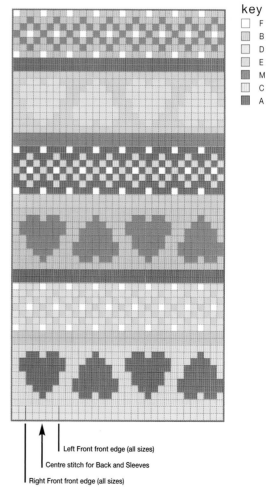

key
F
B
D
E
M
C
A

Left Front front edge (all sizes)
Centre stitch for Back and Sleeves
Right Front front edge (all sizes)

dots & stripes blanket

A blanket is the perfect gift for a newborn baby. Ideal for boys or girls and in lightweight yarn, it will become a much-loved heirloom and be cherished for years.

materials

4 50g/1¾oz balls of Rowan *4 ply Soft* in main colour **M** (lilac/Buzz 375), 2 balls each in **A** (lime green/Goblin 379) and **B** (turquoise/Splash 373) and one ball in **C** (white/Nippy 376)
Pair of long 3¼mm(US 3) knitting needles

size

Approximately 62cm/24½in by 87cm/34¼in.

tension/gauge

28 sts and 36 rows to 10cm/4in over st-st using 3¼mm(US 3) needles

abbreviations

beg beginning; **cm** centimetre(s);
in inch(es); **k** knit; **p** purl; **RS** right side;
st(s) stitch(es); **st-st** stocking/
stockinette stitch

note

The squares are all worked in st-st beg with a RS (k) row and have 7 moss/seed sts in M between each square and 3cm/1¼in in moss/seed st between each line of squares. Spot squares are worked from two charts (small spots and large spots) and in nine colour combinations. Use separate small balls of yarn for each spot square, twisting yarns at colour change to avoid holes.

squares patterns
striped squares
Worked over 25 sts and 32 rows.

Stripe square 1 – 2 rows C, 4 rows B, 3 rows A, 4 rows C, 5 rows M, 3 rows B, 4 rows C, 4 rows A, 3 rows B.

Stripe square 2 – 4 rows A, 6 rows B, 2 rows C, 5 rows M, 3 rows A, 4 rows C, 4 rows M, 4 rows B.

large and small spot squares
Worked over 25 sts and 32 rows.

Spot square 1 – Background in C with spots in M.
Spot square 2 – Background in A with spots in M.
Spot square 3 – Background in B with spots in C.
Spot square 4 – Background in B with spots in M.
Spot square 5 – Background in A with spots in B.
Spot square 6 – Background in A with spots in C.
Spot square 7 – Background in C with spots in B.
Spot square 8 – Background in C with spots in A.
Spot square 9 – Background in B with spots in A.

to make
With 3¼mm(US 3) needles and M, cast on 175 sts.
Moss/seed st row K1, [p1, k1] to end.
This last row forms moss/seed st and is repeated.
Work 4cm/1½in in moss/seed st, ending with a WS row.
first line of squares
Next row (RS) K1, [p1, k1] 5 times, k 25 sts of first row of *large spot square 1*, k1M, [p1M, k1M] 3 times, k25 sts of first row of *stripe square 1*, moss/seed st 7 in M, k first row of *large spot square 2*, moss/seed st 7M, k first row *stripe square 1*, moss/seed st 7M, k first row of *large spot square 3*, moss/seed st 11M.

This last row sets the position of the first line of large spot and stripe 1 squares with 7 moss/seed sts in M between squares and 11-st moss/seed st borders in M at each edge.

When all 32 rows of first line of squares have been worked, work 3cm/1¼in in moss/seed st in M, ending with a WS row. (**Note** Always end horizontal bands of moss/seed st with a WS row, so RS will be facing for starting next line of squares.)

Cont to work moss/seed st borders in M, work 6 more lines of squares with 3cm/1¼in of moss/seed st in M between them, working squares in each line as foll:
2nd line of squares
Stripe square 2, small spot square 4, stripe square 2, small spot square 1, stripe square 2.
3rd line of squares
Large spot square 5, stripe square 1, large spot square 3, stripe square 1, large spot square 2.
4th line of squares
Stripe square 2, small spot square 6, stripe square 2, small spot square 7, stripe square 2.
5th line of squares
Large spot square 4, stripe square 1, large spot square 8, stripe square 1, large spot square 9.
6th line of squares
Stripe square 2, small spot square 3, stripe square 2, small spot square 6, stripe square 2.
7th line of squares
Large spot square 2, stripe square 1, large spot square 9, stripe square 1, large spot square 1.

When 7th line of squares has been worked, work 4cm/1½in in moss/seed st in M.
Cast/bind off in moss/seed st.

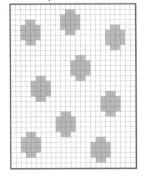

small spot chart

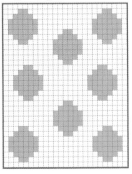

large spot chart

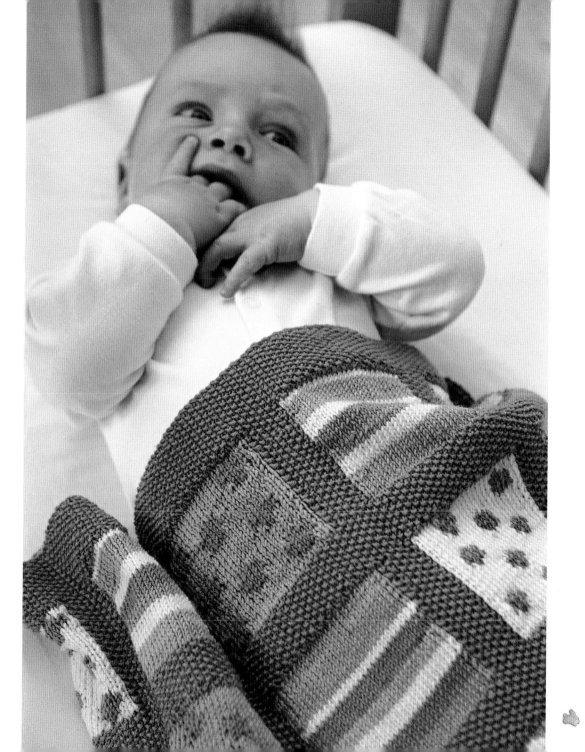

🐰 fun to wear

funky tank top

This cotton top looks great in bright colours or muted tones. Experiment with your own colourways to find a combination that will suit your own funky monkey.

materials

2 50g/1¾oz balls of Rowan *Handknit DK Cotton* in **A** (blue/Galaxy 308 or brown/Tope 253) and one ball each in **B** (red/Rosso 215 or sea green/Nautical 311), **C** (orange/Flame 254 or light sea green/Ice Water 239), **D** (yellow/Sunflower 304 or off-white/Ecru 251), **E** (lime green/ Gooseberry 219 or green/Foggy 301) and **F** (turquoise/Oasis 202 or beige/Linen 205)

Pair each of 3¾mm(US 5) and 4mm(US 6) knitting needles

tension/gauge

20 sts and 28 rows to 10cm/4in over st-st using 4mm(US 6) needles

abbreviations

beg beginning; **cm** centimetre(s); **cont** continu(e)(ing); **dec** decrease; **foll** follow(s)(ing); **in** inch(es); **k** knit; **p** purl; **patt** pattern; **rem** remaining; **rep** repeat; **RS** right side; **sl** slip; **st(s)** stitch(es); **st-st** stocking/stockinette stitch; **tog** together; **WS** wrong side

sizes

to fit

6–12 mths	1–2	2–3	3–4	yrs
actual measurements				
chest				
56	61	66	71	cm
22	24	26	28	in
length				
30	33	36	38	cm
11¾	13	14	15	in

stripe sequence

12 rows B, 9 rows C, 8 rows A, 3 rows D, 9 rows E,
7 rows F, 8 rows C, 6 rows B, 9 rows D, 4 rows A,
10 rows F, 10 rows E

back

With 3¼mm(US 5) needles and A, cast on
56(60:66:70) sts.
1st row (RS) K2(0:2:0), p2(1:2:1), [k3, p2]
10(11:12:13) times, k2(3:2:3), p0(1:0:1).
2nd row (WS) P2(0:2:0), k2(1:2:1), [p3, k2]
10(11:12:13) times, p2(3:2:3), k0(1:0:1).
Rep last 2 rows 4(4:5:5) times more and first row
again, so ending with a RS row.
P 1 row.
Change to 4mm(US 6) needles and B.
Beg with a RS (k) row, work 38(44:48:52) rows in
st-st in stripe sequence.
shape armholes
Keeping stripe sequence correct, cast/bind off 4(4:5:5)
sts at beg of next 2 rows, then dec 1 st at
each end of next row and 3 foll RS rows. 40(44:48:52)
sts.**
Cont straight in striped st-st for 23(25:29:31) rows
more.
shape back neck
Next row (RS) K10(11:12:14), turn and cont on
these sts only, leaving rem sts on a spare needle.
Cast/bind off 2 sts at beg of next row.
Cast/bind off rem 8(9:10:12) sts.
With RS facing, slip 20(22:24:24) sts at centre back
onto a holder, rejoin yarn to rem sts and k to end.
P 1 row.
Cast/bind off 2 sts at beg of next row.
Cast/bind off rem 8(9:10:12) sts.

front

Work as for Back to **.
Cont straight in striped st-st for 11(13:17:19) rows
more.

shape front neck
Next row (RS) K15(16:17:19), turn and cont on
these sts only, leaving rem sts on a spare needle.
Cast/bind off 2 sts at beg (neck edge) of next and foll
WS row, then dec 1 st at beg of 3 foll WS rows.
8(9:10:12) sts.
Work 4 rows more.
Cast/bind off.
With RS facing, slip 10(12:14:14) sts at centre front
onto a holder, rejoin yarn to rem sts and complete to
match first side, reversing shaping.

neckband

Join right shoulder.
With RS facing, 3¼mm(US 5) needles and A, pick up
and k 14 sts down left front neck, k across
10(12:14:14) sts at centre front, pick up and k 14 sts
up right front neck, 2 sts at right back neck, k across
20(22:24:24) sts at centre back, then pick up and k 2
sts up left back neck. 62(66:70:70) sts.
1st row (WS) P2(1:0:0), [k2, p3] 12(13:14:14) times.
2nd row (RS) [K3, p2] 12(13:14:14) times,
k2(1:0:0).
Rep last 2 rows twice more.
Cast/bind off in patt.

armbands

Join left shoulder and neckband seam.
With RS facing, 3¼mm(US 5) needles and A, pick up
and k 72(76:86:90) sts around armhole edge.
1st row (WS) K2(0:0:1), p3(2:2:3), [k2, p3]
13(14:16:17) times, k2(2:2:1), p0(2:2:0).
2nd row (RS) P2(0:0:1), k3(2:2:3), [p2, k3]
13(14:16:17) times, p2(2:2:1), k0(2:2:0).
Rep last 2 rows once more.
Cast/bind off in patt

to finish

Join side and armband seams.

sundress

This knitted dress is cool to wear and stylish too. Its bold design was inspired by a day at the seaside – striped deckchairs and old-fashioned swimming costumes.

materials

2(3:3:3) 50g/1¾oz balls of Rowan *Cotton Glacé* in main colour **M** (red/ Poppy 741) and 2 balls in **A** (off-white/Ecru 725)
Pair each of 2¾mm(US 2) and 3¼mm(US 3) needles
2 buttons

sizes

to fit

6–12 mths	1–2	2–3	3–4	yrs
actual measurements				
chest at underarm				
56	61	65	70	cm
22	24	26	28	in
length to shoulder (adjustable)				
41	45	49	53	cm
16	17¾	19¼	20¾	in

tension/gauge

23 sts and 32 rows to 10cm/4in over st-st using 3¼mm(US 3) needles

abbreviations

alt alternate; **beg** begin(ning); **cm** centimetre(s); **cont** continu(e)(ing); **dec** decrease; **foll** follow(s)(ing); **in** inch(es); **k** knit; **p** purl; **rem** remaining; **rep** repeat; **RS** right side; **sl** slip; **ssk** sl 1 knitwise, sl 1 knitwise, insert tip of left needle through fronts of both slipped sts and k2tog through back of loops; **st(s)** stitch(es); **st-st** stocking/stockinette stitch; **tog** together; **WS** wrong side

back and front (both alike)

With 2¾mm(US 2) needles and M, cast on 91(99:105:113) sts.

Moss/seed st row K1, [p1, k1] to end.

This row forms moss/seed st and is repeated.

Work 3cm/1¼in in moss/seed st.

Change to 3¼mm(US 3) needles.

Beg with a RS (k) row work in 8-row st-st stripe repeat of 4 rows C, 4 rows M.

Work 4 rows, so ending with a WS (p) row in C.

Keeping st-st stripe sequence (4 rows C, 4 rows M) correct throughout, beg shaping on next row as foll:

Dec row (RS) K5, ssk, k to last 7 sts, k2tog, k5.

Work 5 rows.

Rep last 6 rows 11(12:13:14) times more, so ending with a WS row. 67(73:77:83) sts.

shape yoke

Cast/bind off 5(5:6:6) sts at beg of next 2 rows and 4(5:4:5) sts at beg of foll 2 rows, so ending with a WS row. 49(53:57:61) sts.

Next row (RS) K1, ssk, k to last 3 sts, k2tog, k1.

Work 1 row.

Rep last 2 rows, 3 times more.

Work 2 rows.

Next row (RS) K1, ssk, k to last 3 sts, k2tog, k1.

Work 1 row.

Rep last 4 rows, 3(4:5:6) times more, so ending with a WS row.

Work 4 rows.

Leave rem 33(35:37:39) sts on a holder.

armhole edging

Join side seams, matching stripes.

With RS facing, 2¾mm(US 2) needles and M, pick up and k 79(85:91:103) sts around armhole edge.

Work 4 rows in moss/seed st.

Cast/bind off purlwise while working p1, then [p2tog, p1] to end.

front yoke edging

With RS facing, 2¾mm(US 2) needles and M, pick up and k 3 sts across row ends of armhole edging, k across 33(35:37:39) sts on front holder, then pick up and k 3 sts across row ends of armhole edging. 39(41:43:45) sts.

Work 4 rows in moss/seed st.

Cast/bind off purlwise while working p1, then [p2tog, p1] to end.

back yoke edging and straps

With RS facing, 2¾mm(US 2) needles and M, pick up and k 3 sts across row ends of armhole edging, k across 33(35:37:39) sts on back holder, then pick up and k 3 sts across row ends of armhole edging. 39(41:43:45) sts.

Work 5 rows in moss/seed st.

divide for straps

Next row (RS) Moss/seed st 18(19:20:21), work 2tog, turn and cont on these 19(20:21:22) sts only, leaving rem sts on a spare needle.

**Dec 1 st at beg of next and 7(8:7:8) foll alt rows. 11(11:13:13) sts.

Cont straight in moss/seed st until strap measures 6(7:8:9)cm/2½(2¾:3¼:3½)in (adjust length here to suit), ending with a WS row.

1st buttonhole row (RS) Moss/seed st 3(3:4:4), cast/bind off 3 sts, moss/seed st to end.

2nd buttonhole row Work in moss/seed st and cast on 3 sts over cast-/bound-off sts in previous row.

Work 4 rows more in moss/seed st.

Cast/bind off in moss/seed st.**

With RS facing, rejoin yarn to rem sts and moss/seed st to end.

Work 1 row in moss/seed st.

Work as first strap from ** to **.

to finish

Sew buttons to front yoke to match buttonholes.

pirate sweater

An eye-catching skull and crossbones sweater will be a firm favourite with any would-be pirate.

materials

3(3:4:4) 50g/1¾oz balls of Rowan *Handknit DK Cotton* in main colour **M** (navy blue/Turkish Plum 277) and 2 balls each in **A** (red/Rosso 215) and **B** (off-white/Ecru 251)

Pair each of 3 ¼mm(US 5) and 4mm(US 6) knitting needles

sizes

to fit

6–12 mths	1–2	2–3	3–4	yrs

actual measurements

chest

56	61	66	71	cm
22	24	26	28	in

length

30	33	36	38	cm
11¼	13	14	15	in

sleeve seam

18	21	23	28	cm
7	8¼	9	11	in

tension/gauge

20 sts and 28 rows to 10cm/4in over st-st using 4mm(US 6) needles

abbreviations

alt alternate; **beg** beginning; **cm** centimetre(s); **cont** continu(e)(ing); **dec** decrease; **foll** follow(s)(ing); **in** inch(es); **inc** increase; **k** knit; **p** purl; **rem** remaining; **rep** repeat; **RS** right side; **st(s)** stitch(es); **st-st** stocking/stockinette stitch; **WS** wrong side

note

When working from chart, use separate small balls of yarn for motif, twisting yarns at colour change to avoid holes.

back

With 3¾mm(US 5) needles and M, cast on
56(60:66:70) sts.

Change to A and k 1 row.

Now work in rib as foll:

1st rib row (WS) P1(1:2:2), k2, [p2, k2] to last
1(1:2:2) sts, p1(1:2:2).

2nd rib row (RS) K1(1:2:2), p2, [k2, p2] to last
1(1:2:2) sts, k1(1:2:2).

Rep last 2 rows until rib measures 3(4:4:5)cm/
1¼(1½:1½:2)in from cast-on edge, ending with a 1st rib
row.**

Change to 4mm(US 6) needles and M.***

Beg with a RS (k) row, work 72(78:84:90) rows in
st-st, so ending with a WS row.

shape back neck

Next row (RS) K16(17:20:21) sts, turn and cont on
these sts only, leaving rem sts on a spare needle.

Cont in st-st, cast/bind off 2 sts at beg of next row.

Cast/bind off rem 14(15:18:19) sts.

With RS facing, slip 24(26:26:28) sts at centre onto a
holder, rejoin yarn to rem sts and k to end.

P 1 row.

Cont in st-st, cast/bind off 2 sts at beg of next row.

Cast/bind off rem 14(15:18:19) sts.

front

Work as for Back to ***.

Beg with a RS (k) row, work 8(12:14:18) rows in st-st,
so ending with a WS (p) row.

place motif

Next row (RS) K5(7:10:12)M, k across 46 sts of first
row of chart, k5(7:10:12)M.

Cont in st-st foll chart until all 50 chart rows have been
worked.

Cont in st-st in M only, work 2(4:8:10) rows.

shape neck

Next row (RS) K22(23:26:27) sts, turn and cont on
these sts only, leaving rem sts on a spare needle.

****Cast/bind off 3 sts at beg (neck edge) of next row,

2 sts at beg of foll 2 alt rows and then dec 1 st at beg of next alt row. 14(15:18:19) sts.

Work 6 rows.

Cast/bind off.

With RS facing, slip 12(14:14:16) sts at centre front onto a holder, rejoin yarn to rem sts and k to end.

P 1 row.

Complete as first side from **** to end.

sleeves

With 3¼mm(US 5) needles and B, cast on 24(28:30:34) sts.

Change to M and work rib as for Back from ** to **.

Change to 4mm(US 6) needles and A.

Beg with a RS (k) row, work in 16-row st-st stripe repeat of 8 rows A, 8 rows B **and at the same time** inc 1 st at each end of every foll 3rd(3rd:4th:4th) row until there are 48(50:54:56) sts.

Cont straight in stripes as set until sleeve measures 18(21:23:28)cm/7(8¼:9:11)in from cast-on edge, ending with a WS row.

Cast/bind off.

neckband

Join right shoulder seam.

With RS facing, 3¼mm(US 5) needles and B, pick up and k 15 sts down left front neck, k across 12(14:14:16) sts at centre front, pick up and k 16 sts up right front neck, 2 sts down right back neck, k across 24(26:26:28) sts at back neck and dec 1 st in centre, then pick up and k 2 sts up left back neck. 70(74:74:78) sts.

1st rib row (WS) P2, [k2, p2] to end.

2nd rib row (RS) K2, [p2, k2] to end.

Rep last 2 rows twice more, then first row again.

Cast/bind off in M.

to finish

Join left shoulder and neckband seam. Matching centre of cast/bound-off edge of sleeve to shoulder, sew on sleeves. Join side and sleeve seams.

skull and crossbones chart

key

☐ B

■ M

strawberries & cream sweater

The inspiration for this sweater is a classic summer dessert, strawberries and cream. The cream cotton knit features a pretty border of strawberries and vivid red edging.

materials

5(6:7) 50g/1¾oz balls of Rowan *Handknit DK Cotton* in main colour **M** (off-white/Ecru 251), one ball in **A** (red/Rosso 215) and small amount each in **B** (navy blue/Turkish plum 277) and **C** (lime green/Gooseberry 219)

Pair each of 3¾mm(US 5) and 4mm(US 6) knitting needles

sizes

to fit

1–2	3–4	5–6	yrs

actual measurements

chest

69	76	82	cm
27	30	32¼	in

length

36	41	47	cm
14¼	16¼	18½	in

sleeve seam

22	28	31	cm
8½	11	12	in

tension/gauge

20 sts and 28 rows to 10cm/4in over st-st using 4mm(US 6) needles

abbreviations

alt alternate; **beg** beginning; **cm** centimetres; **cont** continu(e)(ing); **dec** decrease; **foll** follow(s)(ing); **in** inch(es); **inc** increase; **k** knit; **p** purl; **rem** remaining; **rep** repeat; **RS** right side; **st(s)** stitch(es); **st-st** stocking/stockinette stitch; **WS** wrong side

note

When working zigzag patt from charts, strand yarn not in use across WS of work. When working motifs from charts, use separate small balls of A, B and C, twisting yarns at colour change to avoid holes. Do not work part motifs on 1st size.

back

**With 3¼mm(US 5) needles and A, cast on 68(76:84) sts.

Change to M and k 1 row.

Rib row [K2, p2] to end.

Rep last row 8 times more.

Change to 4mm(US 6) needles and beg with a RS (k) row, work 21 rows in st-st from strawberry border chart, so ending with a RS (k) row.

Beg with a p row and cont in st-st in M only, work 39(43:49) rows more, so ending with a WS row.

shape armholes

Cast/bind off 4(5:5) sts at beg of next 2 rows. 60(66:74) sts.**

Cont straight for 32(40:52) rows more, so ending with a WS row.

shape back neck

Next row (RS) K19(21:24), turn and p to end.

Cast/bind off.

With RS facing, slip centre 22(24:26) sts onto a holder, rejoin yarn to rem sts and k to end.

P 1 row.

Cast/bind off.

front

Work as for Back from ** to **.

Cont straight for 20(26:36) rows more, so ending with a WS row.

shape front neck

Next row (RS) K26(29:32), turn and cont on these sts only, leaving rem sts on a spare needle.

Cast/bind off 3 sts at beg of next row.

Dec 1 st at neck edge on next 4(2:3) rows, then dec 1 st at neck edge on foll 0(3:2) alt rows. 19(21:24) sts.

Cont straight for 8(6:9) rows more.

Cast/bind off.

With RS facing, slip 8(8:10) sts at centre front onto a holder, rejoin yarn to rem sts and k to end.

P 1 row.

Cast/bind off 3 sts at beg of next row.

Dec 1 st at neck edge on next 4(2:3) rows, then dec 1 st at neck edge on foll 0(3:2) alt rows. 19(21:24) sts.

Cont straight for 7(5:8) rows more.

Cast/bind off.

sleeves

With 3¾mm(US 5) needles and A, cast on 36(38:40) sts.
Change to M and k 1 row.

1st and 3rd sizes only

Work 7 rows in rib as for Back.

2nd size only

1st rib row K2, [p2, k2] to end.
2nd rib row P2 [k2, p2] to end.
Rep last 2 rows twice more and then first rib row again.
Change to 4mm(US 6) needles and beg with a RS (k) row,
work 21 rows in st st from sleeve chart **and at the same
time** inc 1 st at each end of 5th and every foll 4th row as
shown, then work in M only and cont to inc as before until
there are 60(68:80) sts.
Cont straight for 11(11:5) rows more.
Cast/bind off.

neckband

Join right shoulder.
With RS facing, 3¾mm(US 5) needles and M, pick up and k
18(20:21) sts down left front neck, k across 8(8:10) sts at
centre front, pick up and k 18(20:21) sts up right front neck,
2 sts down right back neck, k across 22(24:26) sts at centre
back and pick up and k 2 sts up left back neck. 70(76:82) sts.
Work in 5 rows in k2, p2 rib as for 2nd size sleeve.
Change to A and rib 1 row as set, then cast/bind off using a
4mm(US 6) needle.

to finish

Join left shoulder and neckband seam. Matching centre of
cast/bound-off edge of sleeve to shoulder, sew sleeve into
armhole. Join side and sleeve seams.

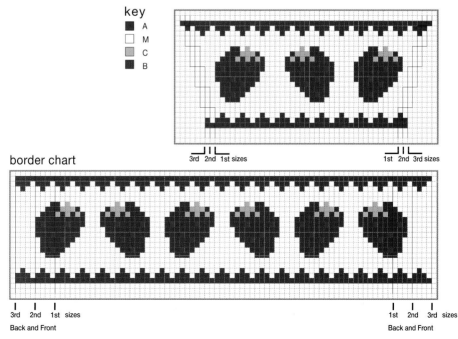

key

■ A
□ M
▨ C
■ B

sleeve chart

3rd 2nd 1st sizes   1st 2nd 3rd sizes

border chart

3rd   2nd   1st sizes   1st   2nd   3rd sizes
Back and Front   Back and Front

heart-motif cardigan

Every little girl will love this cardigan. The contrast-edged frilled detailing gives it the perfect finish.

materials

5(5:6:6) 50g/1¾oz balls of Rowan *Handknit DK Cotton* in main colour **M** (blue/Diana 287) and one ball each in **A** (pink/Sugar 303), **B** (lilac/Lupin 305), **C** (orange/Flame 251), **D** (red/Rosso 215), **E** (yellow/Sunshine 304) and **F** (lime green/Lush 306)

Pair each of 3¼mm(US 5) and 4mm(US 6) knitting needles

5 buttons

sizes

to fit

6–12 mths	1–2	2–3	3–4	yrs
actual measurements				
chest				
56	61	66	71	cm
22	24	26	28	in
length				
30	33	36	38	cm
11¼	13	14	15	in
sleeve seam				
18	21	23	26	cm
7	8	9	10	in

tension/gauge

20 sts and 28 rows to 10cm/4in over st-st using 4mm(US 6) needles

abbreviations

alt alternate; **beg** beginning; **cm** centimetre(s); **cont** continu(e)(ing); **dec** decrease; **foll** follow(s)(ing); **in** inch(es); **inc** increase; **k** knit; **p** purl; **patt** pattern; **psso** pass slipped st over; **rem** remaining; **rep** repeat; **RS** right side; **skpo** sl 1, k1, psso; **sl** slip; **sts** stitch(es); **st-st** stocking/stockinette stitch; **tog** together; **WS** wrong side; **yrn (yarn round needle)** wrap yarn around right needle from front to back and to front again between needles to make a st

note

When working from charts, use a separate small ball of yarn for each motif, twisting yarns at colour change to avoid holes. When working sleeves, do not work incomplete heart motifs.

back

With 4mm(US 6) needles and A, cast on 140(152:162:180) sts.
Change to M.

1st row (WS) P.

2nd row (RS) P2(3:3:2), [skpo, k3, k2tog, p3] to last
8(9:9:8) sts, skpo, k3, k2tog, p1(2:2:1).

3rd row K all k sts and p all p sts.

4th row P2(3:3:2), [skpo, k1, k2tog, p3] to last 6(7:7:6) sts,
skpo, k1, k2tog, p1(2:2:1).

5th row As 3rd row.

6th row P2(3:3:2), [sl 1, k2tog, psso, p3] to last 4(5:5:4) sts,
sl 1, k2tog, psso, p1(2:2:1).

7th row K1(2:2:1), [p1, k3] to last 3(4:4:3) sts, p1,
k2(3:3:2). 56(62:66:72) sts.

Beg with a RS (k) row and starting on chart row 5(3:1:1),
work in st-st from chart, working between lines for correct
size.

Cast/bind off sts for armhole and back neck shaping where
shown, and cast/bind off back neck sts.

pocket lining (make 1)

With 4mm(US 6) needles and M, cast on 15(17:17:19) sts.
Beg with a RS (k) row, work 20(20:22:22) rows in st-st.
Leave sts on a holder.

left front

With 4mm(US 6) needles and A, cast on 79(88:90:99) sts.
Change to M.

1st row (WS) P.

2nd row (RS) P2(1:3:2), [skpo, k3, k2tog, p3] to last 7sts,
skpo, k3, k2tog.

3rd row K all k sts and p all p sts.

4th row P2(1:3:2), [skpo, k1, k2tog, p3] to last 5 sts, skpo,
k1, k2tog.

5th row As 3rd row.

6th row P2(1:3:2), [sl 1, k2tog, psso, p3] to last 3 sts, sl 1,
k2tog, psso.

7th row (WS) [P1, k3] to last 3(2:4:3) sts, p1, k2(1:3:2).
31(34:36:39) sts.

Next row (RS) K26(29:31:34), [k1, p1] twice, k1.

Next row (WS) K1, [p1, k1] twice, p to end.

These last 2 rows set the position for the st-st with moss/seed st button band.

Keeping the st-st and moss/seed st as set, work from chart (only the st-st areas are shown) until 20(20:22:22) st-st chart rows have been worked.

place pocket

Next row (RS) K8(9:11:12), slip next 15(17:17:19) sts onto a holder for pocket top, k across 15(17:17:19) sts of pocket lining, k3, moss/seed st 5.

Cont to work from chart until chart row 68(74:80:86) has been worked.

shape neck

Next row (RS) Patt to last 5 sts and slip these rem 5 moss/seed sts onto a safety pin.

Complete foll chart, working neck shaping as shown.

Mark the position of 5 buttons on the moss/seed st button band, the first directly above the lower frill, the last just below the neck shaping and the rem 3 spaced evenly between.

right front

With 4mm(US 6) needles and A, cast on 79(88:90:99) sts. Change to M.

1st row (WS) P.

2nd row (RS) [Skpo, k3, k2tog, p3] to last 9(8:10:9) sts, skpo, k3, k2tog, p2(1:3:2).

3rd row K all k sts and p all p sts.

4th row [Skpo, k1, k2tog, p3] to last 7(6:8:7) sts, skpo, k1, k2tog, p2(1:3:2).

5th row As 3rd row.

6th row [Sl 1, k2tog, psso, p3] to last 5(4:6:5) sts, sl 1, k2tog, psso, p2(1:3:2).

7th row (WS) K2(1:3:2), p1, [k3, p1] to end. 31(34:36:39) sts.

Buttonhole row (RS) K1, p1, yrn, p2tog, k1, k to end.

Next row (WS) P to last 5 sts, [k1, p1] twice, k1.

Next row (RS) K1, [p1, k1] twice, k to end.

The last 2 rows set the position for the st-st with moss/seed st buttonhole band.

Keeping the st-st and moss/seed st as set, work from chart

(only the st-st areas are shown), working buttonholes on RS rows as before, to match button markers, until chart row 69(75:81:87) has been worked.

Next row (WS) Patt to last 5 sts and slip rem 5 moss/seed-sts onto a safety pin.

Complete foll chart, working neck shaping as shown.

sleeves

With 4mm(US 6) needles and A, cast on 75(75:85:85) sts. Change to M.

1st row (WS) P.

2nd row (RS) P4, [skpo, k3, k2tog, p3] to last st, p1.

3rd row K all k sts and p all p sts.

4th row P4, [skpo, k1, k2tog, p3] to last st, p1.

5th row As 3rd row.

6th row P4, [sl 1, k2tog, psso, p3] to last st, p1.

7th row (WS) K1, [k3, p1] to last 4 sts, k4. 33(33:37:37) sts.

Beg with a RS (k) row on chart row 3(1:1:1) and working in st-st from chart within lines for correct size, inc 1 st at each end of 5th(7th:7th:7th) row, then on foll 4th and 6th rows alternately for 1st and 2nd sizes only and every foll 6th row for 3rd and 4th sizes only, until there are 49(51:55:57) sts.

Cont straight until chart row 46(52:56:64) has been worked. Mark each end of last row, then work 6 rows more.

Cast/bind off.

pocket top

With RS facing, 3¾mm(US 5) needles and M, k
across 15(17:17:19) sts of pocket.
Work 4 rows in moss/seed st.
Cast/bind off in moss/seed st.

collar

Join shoulder seams.
With WS facing, 3¾mm(US 5) needles and M,
moss/seed st across 5 sts on safety pin at right
front.
Next row (RS) Cast/bind off 2 sts, moss/seed
st rem 2 sts, pick up and k 16(16:17:17) sts up
right front neck, 22(24:26:28) sts around back
neck, 17(17:18:18) sts down left front neck,
then moss/seed st across 5 sts on left front safety
pin.
Next row (WS) Cast/bind off 2 sts, moss/seed
st to end. 61(63:67:69) sts.
Cont in moss/seed st until collar measures
2cm/¾in.
Change to 4mm(US 6) needles and work
5cm/2in more in moss/seed st.
Cast/bind off in moss/seed st.

to finish

Sew sleeves into armholes, joining row ends
above markers to cast-/bound-off sts at underarm. Join side, sleeve and edging seams. Slipstitch pocket lining and top in place.

sleeve chart

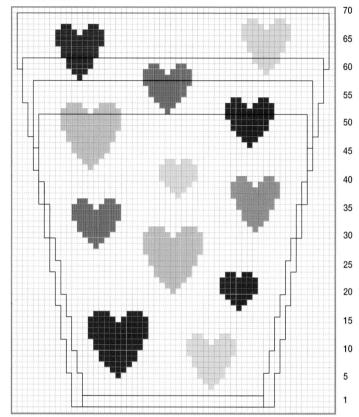

key

back and front chart

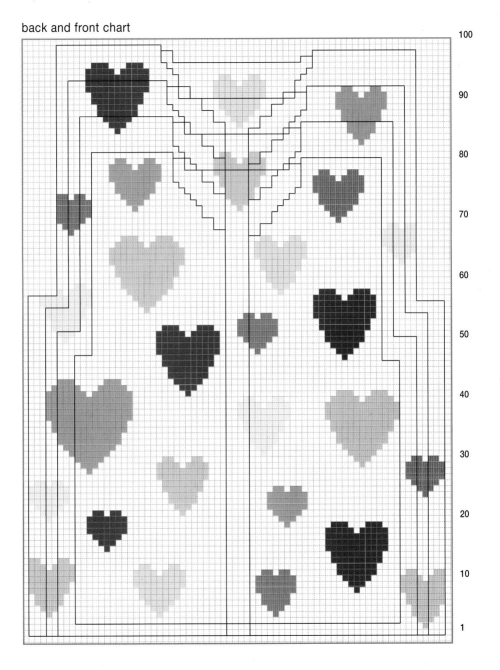

fairy dress

What could be more fun than being a fairy or princess? The simple bodice with pretty ribbon ties and net skirt make this the ideal outfit for every special occasion.

materials

1(1:2:2) 50g/1¾oz balls of Jaeger *Aqua* in
   main colour **M** (hot pink/India 322) and
   one ball in **A** (lilac/Comfrey 328)
Pair of 3¼mm(US 5) knitting needles
   3¼mm(US 5) circular needle
1m/1yd each of dark pink, pale pink and lilac
   net fabric
2m/2yd of 15mm-/½in-wide pink ribbon
waist length of 5mm-/¼in-wide elastic
Sewing thread

sizes

to fit

6–12 mths	1–2	3–4	4–5	yrs
actual measurements				
chest				
45	54	57	61	cm
17¾	21¼	22½	24	in

tension/gauge

22 sts and 30 rows to 10cm/4in over st-st using 3¼mm(US 5) needles

abbreviations

alt alternate; **beg** beginning; **cm** centimetre(s); **cont** continu(e)(ing); **dec** decrease; **foll** follow(s)(ing); **in** inch(es); **k** knit; **p** purl; **patt** pattern; **rem** remaining; **RS** right side; **st(s)** stitch(es); **st-st** stocking/stockinette stitch; **tog** together; **WS** wrong side

bodice back

With 3¾mm (US 5) needles and A, cast on 49(59:63:67) sts.

K 1 row.

Change to M and work in patt as foll:

1st row (RS) K12(15:16:17), p1, [k1, p1] 12(14:15:16) times, k12(15:16:17).

2nd row (WS) P12(15:16:17), k1, [p1, k1] 12(14:15:16) times, p12(15:16:17).

These last 2 rows form the patt and are repeated.

Cont in patt until bodice back measures 13(14:15:16)cm/5(5½:6:6¼)in from cast-on edge, ending with a WS row.

shape armhole

Cast/bind off 3(3:4:4) sts at beg of next 2 rows and 2 sts at beg of foll 2(6:6:6) rows, then dec 1 st at each end of next and foll 2(1:1:2) alt rows. 33(37:39:41) sts.

P 1 row.

shape neck

Next row (RS) K7, turn and cont on these sts only, leaving rem sts on a spare needle.

Cast/bind off 3 sts at beg (neck edge) of next row and 2 sts at beg of foll alt row. 2 sts.

K1 row.

P2tog and fasten off.

With RS facing, slip 19(23:25:27) sts at centre onto a holder, rejoin yarn to 7 rem sts and complete to match first side.

bodice front

With 3¾mm(US 5) needles and A, cast on 49(59:63:67) sts.

K 1 row.

Change to M and work as for Back, but in st-st only.

edging

Join right side seam.

With RS facing, 3¾mm(US 5) circular needle and A, pick up and k 18(22:23:25) sts up left front armhole edge, 8 sts down left front neck, k across 19(23:25:27) sts at centre front, pick up and k 8 sts up right front neck, 36(44:46:50) sts around right armhole edge, 8 sts down right back neck, k across 19(23:25:27) sts at centre back, then pick up and k 8 sts up left back neck and 18(22:23:25) sts down left back armhole edge. 142(166:174:186) sts.

Cast/bind off knitwise.

Join left side seam. Cut ribbon into four lengths and stitch to back and front of the bodice.

skirt

Following the illustration below, cut the net into petal shapes. Place the layers over each other and fold the straight edges over, running a line of stitching along to hold them in place. Thread elastic through the hem to form a skirt and stitch the ends of elastic together. Then stitch to the lower edge of the bodice.

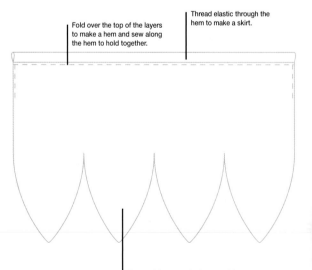

Fold over the top of the layers to make a hem and sew along the hem to hold together.

Thread elastic through the hem to make a skirt.

Cut petal shapes at the bottom of the net.

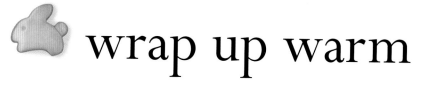 wrap up warm

ship ahoy! sweater

This nautical knitted sweater, with boat and fishes, looks jolly and is lovely and comfortable too.

materials

3(4:4:5) 50g/1¾oz balls of Rowan *Cotton Glacé* in main colour **M** (blue/Splendour 810) and one ball each in **A** (red/Poppy 741) and **B** (yellow/Sunny 802)

One 50g/1¾oz ball each of Jaeger *Aqua* in **C** (navy blue/Deep 320) and **D** (light green/Herb 303)

Pair of 3¼mm(US 3) knitting needles

sizes

to fit

6–12 mths	1–2	2–3	3–4	yrs
actual measurements				
chest				
56	61	66	71	cm
22	24	26	28	in
length				
30	33	36	38	cm
11¼	13	14	15	in
sleeve seam				
18	21	23	27	cm
7	8¼	9	10¾	in

tension/gauge

23 sts and 32 rows to 10cm/4in over st-st using 3¼mm(US 3) needles

abbreviations

alt alternate; **beg** beginning; **cm** centimetre(s); **cont** continu(e)(ing); **dec** decrease; **foll** follow(s)(ing); **in** inch(es); **inc** increase; **k** knit; **p** purl; **patt** pattern; **rem** remaining; **rep** repeat; **RS** right side; **st(s)** stitch(es); **st-st** stocking/stockinette stitch; **tog** together; **WS** wrong side

note

When working from charts, use separate small balls of yarn for each motif, twisting yarns at colour change to avoid holes.

back

With 3¼mm(US 3) needles and C, cast on
64(70:76:82) sts.

Beg with a RS (k) row, work 6 rows in st-st.

Change to M.

1st rib row (RS) K3(2:3:2), [p2, k2] to last 1(0:1:0)
st, k1(0:1:0).

2nd rib row P3(2:3:2), [k2, p2] to last 1(0:1:0) st,
p1(0:1:0).

Rep last 2 rows 3 times more.**

Beg with a RS (k) row, work 48(54:60:64) rows in
st-st.

shape armholes

Cont in st-st, cast/bind off 5 sts at beg of next 2 rows.
54(60:66:72) sts.

Cont straight for 36(38:42:46) rows more.

shape shoulders

Cast/bind off 12(14:16:18) sts at beg of next 2 rows.

Leave rem 30(32:34:36) sts on a holder.

front

Work as for Back to **.

Beg with a RS (k) row, work 6(10:10:12) rows in st-st,
so ending with a WS (p) row.

place fish chart

Next row (RS) K13(16:18:21)M, k across 14 sts of
first row of fish chart, k to end in M.

Cont in st-st foll chart until all 7 chart rows have been
worked.

Cont in st-st in M only for 25(25:39:39) rows more, so
ending with a WS row.

place boat chart

Next row (RS) K20(23:26:29)M, k across 25 sts of
first row of boat chart, k to end in M.

Cont in st-st foll chart until chart row 10(12:4:6) has
been worked.

shape armholes

Keeping chart correct, cast/bind off 5 sts at beg of next
2 rows, then cont straight on rem 54(60:66:72) sts

until all 29 chart rows have been worked.

Cont in st-st in M only for 3(7:3:9) rows more, so
ending with a WS row.

shape neck

Next row (RS) K21(24:27:30), turn and cont on
these sts only, leaving rem sts on a spare needle.

Cast/bind off 3 sts at beg (neck edge) of next row, 2 sts
at beg of foll 1(1:2:3) alt rows and dec 1 st at beg of
next 4(5:4:3) alt rows. 12(14:16:18) sts.

Work 4(2:2:2) rows.

Cast/bind off for shoulder.

With RS facing, slip 12 sts at centre front onto a holder,
rejoin yarn to rem sts and complete to match first side.

left sleeve

With 3¼mm(US 3) needles and C, cast on
28(30:32:34) sts.

Beg with a RS (k) row, work 6 rows in st-st.

Change to M.

1st rib row (RS) K3(2:3:2), [p2, k2] to last 1(0:1:0)
st, k1(0:1:0).

2nd rib row P3(2:3:2), [k2, p2] to last 1(0:1:0) st,
p1(0:1:0).

Rep last 2 rows 3 times more.

Beg with a RS (k) row and working in st-st, inc 1 st at
each end of 3rd(7th:1st:5th) row and foll 2(1:2:1)
3rd(3rd:4th:4th) rows. 34(34:38:38) sts.

Work 1(0:1:1) row, so ending with a WS row.

place fish chart

Next row (RS) K12(12:14:14)M, k across 14 sts of
first row of fish chart, k8(8:10:10)M.

Cont in st-st foll chart until all 7 chart rows have been
worked and **at the same time** cont to inc as set on
next(2nd:2nd:2nd) row and then on every foll
3rd(3rd:4th:4th) row until there are 56(60:64:68) sts.

Cont straight until sleeve measures 18(21:23:27)cm/
7(8¼:9:10¼)in from beg of rib.

Mark each end of last row, then work 6 rows more.

Cast/bind off.

right sleeve

Work as for Left Sleeve, but omitting fish.

neckband

Join right shoulder seam.

With RS facing, 3¼mm(US 3) needles and M, pick up and k 19(19:21:21) sts down left front neck, k across 10 sts at centre front, pick up and k 19(19:21:21) sts up right front neck, then k across 30(32:34:36) sts at back neck and inc 2 sts evenly. 80(82:88:90) sts.

Beg with a 2nd rib row, work 3cm/1¼in in rib as for Back, ending with a 2nd rib row.

Change to C and beg with a RS (k) row, work 6 rows in st-st.

Cast/bind off.

to finish

Join left shoulder and neckband seam. Sew sleeves into armholes, joining row ends above markers to cast-/bound-off sts at underarm. Join side and sleeve seams.

fish motif

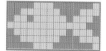

boat motif

key
M
A
D
B
C

ballerina wrap

This ballerina wrap can be jazzed up with a colourful ribbon or toned down with a plain tie. Either way, it looks great worn with a pretty skirt.

materials

3(4:4:5) 50g balls of Debbie Bliss *Baby Cashmerino* in pale blue/Pale Blue 202
Pair each of 3mm(US 2) and 3¼mm(US 3) knitting needles
1m/1yd of 2cm-/¾in-wide ribbon

sizes

to fit

6–12 mths	1–2	2–3	3–4	yrs
actual measurements				
chest				
56	61	66	71	cm
22	24	26	28	in
length				
23	25	28	31	cm
9	9¾	11	12	in
sleeve seam				
18	21	23	28	cm
7	8¼	9	11	in

tension/gauge

25 sts and 34 rows to 10cm/4in over st-st using 3¼mm(US 3) needles

abbreviations

beg beginning; **cm** centimetre(s); **cont** continu(e)(ing); **dec** decrease; **foll** follow(s)(ing); **in** inch(es); **inc** increase; **k** knit; **m1** make one st by picking up and working into back of loop lying between last st and next st; **p** purl; **rem** remaining; **rep** repeat; **RS** right side; **sl** slip; **st(s)** stitch(es); **st-st** stocking/stockinette stitch; **tog** together; **WS** wrong side

back

With 3mm(US 2) needles, cast on 57(65:69:73) sts.
K 2 rows.
Change to 3¼mm(US 3) needles.
Beg with a RS (k) row, work 8 rows in st-st, so ending with a WS (p) row.
Inc row (RS) K2, m1, k to last 2 sts, m1, k2.
Con in st-st, work 5(5:7:7) rows.
Rep last 6(6:8:8) rows 4 times more. 67(75:79:83) sts.
Work 0(4:0:6) rows.
shape armholes
Cast/bind off 4(4:5:5) sts at beg of next 2 rows.
59(67:69:73) sts.
Work 38(42:46:50) rows.
shape shoulders
Cast/bind off 9(10:10:11) sts at beg of next 2 rows and 8(10:10:10) sts at beg of foll 2 rows.
Leave rem 25(27:29:31) sts on a holder.

left front

With 3mm(US 2) needles, cast on 50(58:62:66) sts.
K 2 rows.
Change to 3¼mm(US 3) needles.
Beg with a RS (k) row, work 4 rows in st-st.
shape front slope
Next row (RS) K to last 3 sts, k2tog, k1.
P 1 row.
Rep last 2 rows once more.
Cont in st-st, dec 1 st at front edge as set on every foll RS row and inc 1 st at side edge as for Back on next row and 4 foll 6th(6th:8th:8th) rows.
Cont as set until 38(44:45:46) sts rem, ending with a WS row.
shape armhole
Next row (RS) Cast/bind off 4(4:5:5) sts, k to last 3 sts, k2tog, k1.
Keeping armhole edge straight, cont to dec 1 st at front edge on every foll RS row until 17(20:20:21) sts rem.
Cont straight for 7(5:9:13) rows, so ending with a WS row.

shape shoulders

Cast/bind off 9(10:10:11) sts at beg of next row.

P 1 row.

Cast/bind off rem 8(10:10:10) sts.

right front

With 3mm(US 2) needles, cast on 50(58:62:66) sts.

K 2 rows.

Change to 3¼mm(US 3) needles.

Beg with a RS (k) row, work 4 rows in st-st.

shape front slope

Next row (RS) K1, k2tog, k to end.

P 1 row.

Rep last 2 rows once more.

Cont in st-st, dec 1 st at front edge as set on every foll RS row and inc 1 st at side edge as for Back on next row and 4 foll 6th(6th:8th:8th) rows.

Cont as set until 37(43:44:45) sts rem, ending with a RS row.

shape armhole

Next row (WS) Cast/bind off 4(4:5:5) sts, p to end.

Keeping armhole edge straight, cont to dec 1 st at front edge on every foll RS row until 17(20:20:21) sts rem.

Cont straight for 8(6:10:14) rows, so ending with a RS row.

shape shoulders

Cast/bind off 9(10:10:11) sts at beg of next row.

K 1 row.

Cast/bind off rem 8(10:10:10) sts.

sleeves

With 3mm(US 2) needles, cast on 38(38:42:42) sts.

K 2 rows.

Change to 3¼mm(US 3) needles.

Beg with a RS (k) row, work 4 rows in st-st.

Inc row (RS) K2, m1, k to last 2 sts, m1, k2.

Cont in st-st, work 3 rows.

Rep last 4 rows until there are 58(64:70:74) sts.

Cont straight until sleeve measures 18(21:23:28)cm/7(8¼:9:11)in from cast-on edge,

ending with a RS row.

Mark each end of last row, then work 5(5:7:7) rows more.

Cast/bind off.

front edging

Join shoulder seams.

With RS facing and 3mm(US 2) needles, pick up and k 80(88:98:108) sts up right front edge, k across 25(27:29:31) sts at back neck, then pick up and k 80(88:98:108) sts down left front edge. 185(203:225:247) sts.

K 2 rows.

Cast/bind off knitwise.

to finish

Sew sleeves into armholes, joining row ends above sleeve markers to cast-/bound-off sts of armholes. Join sleeve seams. Join side seams, leaving a 2cm/¾in gap in left seam 1cm/½in above cast-on edge. Sew a 40cm/16in length of ribbon to right front edge below start of front slope shaping and rem 60cm/24in to left front edge.

chunky cabled sweater

The red contrast edging makes this classic cabled sweater a little bit special. The cashmere-blend yarn is warm and cosy and shows up the cables beautifully.

materials

5(6:6:7) 50g/1¾oz balls of Debbie Bliss
    Cashmerino Aran in main colour **M**
    (olive/Khaki 500) and one ball in **A**
    (red/Red 610)
Pair each of 4½mm(US 7) and 5mm(US 8)
    knitting needles
Cable needle

sizes

to fit

6–12 mths	1–2	2–3	3–4	yrs

actual measurements

chest

56	61	66	71	cm
22	24	26	28	in

length

30	33	36	38	cm
11¾	13	14	15	in

sleeve seam

18	21	24	28	cm
7	8¼	9½	11	in

tension/gauge

18 sts and 30 rows to 10cm/4in over
moss/seed st using 5mm(US 8) needles

abbreviations

alt alternate; **beg** beginning; **BC (back cross)**
sl next 3 sts onto cable needle and hold at back,
k2, sl p st from cable needle onto left needle and
p1, k2 from cable needle; **C4B (cable 4 back)**
sl next 2 sts onto cable needle and hold at back,
k2, then k2 from cable needle; **C4F (cable 4
front)** as C4B but hold cable needle in front;
cm centimetre(s); **cont** continu(e)(ing); **dec**
decrease; **FC (front cross)** as BC but hold
cable needle in front; **foll** follow(s)(ing) **in**
inch(es); **inc** increase; **k** knit; **p** purl; **patt**
pattern; **rem** remaining; **rep** repeat; **RS** right
side; **sl** slip; **st(s)** stitch(es); **st-st** stocking/
stockinette stitch; **tog** together; **Tw2L (twist 2
left)** k into back of 2nd st on left needle, k into
front of first st on left needle, sl both sts off
needle; **Tw2R (twist 2 right)** k into front of
2nd st on left needle, k into front of first st on
left needle, sl both sts off needle; **WS** wrong side

note

Work all instructions in [ ]s the number of times stated.

back

With 4½mm(US 7) needles and A, cast on 62(67:72:82) sts.

Change to M.

1st rib row (RS) P2, [k3, p2] to end.

2nd rib row (WS) K2, [p3, k2] to end.

These last 2 rows form rib and are repeated.

Work 4cm/1½in in rib, ending with a 2nd rib row.

Inc row (RS) K and inc 4(11:10:12) sts evenly across row. 66(78:82:94) sts.

Change to 5mm(US 8) needles.

1st row (WS) K1, [p1, k1] 5(3:4:7) times, k1, p2, k1, [k1, p4, k2, p2, k1] 1(2:2:2) times, [k1, p2] 5 times, k1, [k1, p2, k2, p4, k1] 1(2:2:2) times, k1, p2, k1, [k1, p1] 5(3:4:7) times, k1.

2nd row (RS) K1, [p1, k1] 5(3:4:7) times, p1, Tw2R, p1, [p1, k4, p2, Tw2R, p1] 1(2:2:2) times, [p1, k2] 5 times, p1, [p1, Tw2L, p2, k4, p1] 1(2:2:2) times, p1, Tw2L, p1, [k1, p1] 5(3:4:7) times, k1.

3rd row As 1st row.

4th row K1, [p1, k1] 5(3:4:7) times, p1, Tw2R, p1, [p1, C4B, p2, Tw2R, p1] 1(2:2:2) times, p1, k2, [p1, FC] twice, p1, [p1, Tw2L, p2, C4F, p1] 1(2:2:2) times,

p1, Tw2L, p1, [k1, p1] 5(3:4:7) times, k1.

5th row As 1st row.

6th row As 2nd row.

7th row As 1st row.

8th row K1, [p1, k1] 5(3:4:7) times, p1, Tw2R, p1, [p1, C4B, p2, Tw2R, p1] 1(2:2:2) times, [p1, BC] twice, p1, k2, p1, [p1, Tw2L, p2, C4F, p1] 1(2:2:2) times, p1, Tw2L, p1, [k1, p1] 5(3:4:7) times, k1.

These last 8 rows form the patt and are repeated.

Work in patt until Back measures 19(21:23:24)cm/ 7½(8¼:9:9½)in from cast-on edge, ending with a WS row.

shape armholes

Cont in patt, cast/bind off 5 sts at beg of next 2 rows. 56(68:72:84) sts.**

Cont straight in patt until Back measures 30(33:36:38)cm/11¾(13:14:15)in from cast-on edge, ending with a WS row.

shape shoulder

Cast/bind off 13(19:20:26) sts at beg of next 2 rows, working 2 sts tog in centre of each 4-st cable.

Leave rem 30(30:32:32) sts on a holder for back neck.

front

Work as for Back to **.

Cont straight in patt until Front measures 25(28:31:33)cm/9¾(11:12¼:13)in from cast-on edge, ending with a WS row.

shape neck

Next row (RS) Patt 21(27:29:35) sts, turn and cont in patt on these sts only, leaving rem sts on a spare needle.

Cast/bind off 2 sts at beg of next and foll 1(1:2:2) alt rows, then dec 1 st at beg of next 4(4:3:3) alt rows. 13(19:20:26) sts.

Cont straight until Front matches Back to shoulder, ending with a WS row.

Cast/bind off, working 2 sts tog in centre of each 4-st cable.

With RS facing, slip 14 sts at centre front onto a holder, rejoin yarn to rem sts and patt to end.

Complete to match first side, reversing shaping.

sleeves

With 4½mm(US 7) needles and A, cast on 27(32:32:37) sts.

Change to M.

Work 6 rows in rib as for Back.

Inc row (RS) K and inc 5(0:4:3) sts evenly across row. 32(32:36:40) sts.

Change to 5mm(US 8) needles.

1st row (WS) [P1, k1] 2(2:3:4) times, k1, p2, k2, [p2, k1] 5 times, k1, p2, k1, [k1, p1] 2(2:3:4) times.

2nd row (RS) [P1, k1] 2(2:3:4) times, p1, Tw2R, p2, [k2, p1] 5 times, p1, Tw2L, p1, [k1, p1] 2(2:3:4) times.

These last 2 rows set the position of the central lattice cable with twist sts and moss/seed st to each side.

Cont in patt and working the lattice cable as for Back, inc 1 st at each end of 4th and every foll 4th row until there are 52(56:60:64) sts, taking all inc sts into moss/seed st.

Cont straight until Sleeve measures

18(21:24:28)cm/7(8¼:9½:11)in from cast-on edge. Mark each end of last row, then work 6 rows more. Cast/bind off in patt.

neckband

Join right shoulder seam.

With RS facing, 4½mm(US 7) needles and M, pick up and k 18 sts down left front neck, k across 14 sts at centre front, pick up and k 18 sts up right front neck, then k across 30(30:32:32) sts at centre back and inc 2(2:0:0) sts evenly. 82 sts.

1st rib row (WS) K2, [p3, k2] to end.

2nd rib row (RS) P2, [k3, p2] to end.

Rep last 2 rows twice more, then first rib row again. Change to A and cast/bind off in patt.

to finish

Join left shoulder and neckband seam. Sew sleeves into armholes, joining row ends above markers to cast/bound-off armhole stitches. Join side and sleeve seams.

multicolour bobble cardigan

This colourful cardigan was inspired by Mexican textiles.
The bright bobbles decorating the neck, cuffs and hem will
be irresistible to tiny fingers.

materials

4(5:5:6) 50g/1¾oz balls of King Cole
Anti-Tickle Merino DK in main colour **M**
(navy blue/Irish Navy 25) and small
amount each in **A** (royal blue/Royal 21),
B (mauve/Larkspur 13), **C** (yellow/Gold
55), **D** (red/Cherry 29) and **E** (hot pink/
Raspberry 67) and **F** (jade/Green Ice 63)
Pair of 3¾mm(US 5) knitting needles
5(6:6:7) buttons

sizes

to fit

6–12 mths	1–2	2–3	3–4	yrs
actual measurements				
chest				
56	61	66	71	cm
22	24	26	28	in
length				
30	33	36	38	cm
11¼	13	14	15	in
sleeve seam				
18	21	23	28	cm
7	8¼	9	11	in

tension/gauge

23 sts and 32 rows to 10cm/4in over st-st
using 3¾mm(US 5) needles

abbreviations

beg beginning; **cm** centimetre(s); **cont**
continu(e)(ing); **dec** decrease; **foll**
follow(s)(ing); **in** inch(es); **inc** increase;
k knit; **p** purl; **patt** pattern; **rem** remaining;
rep repeat; **RS** right side; **sl** slip; **st(s)**
stitch(es); **st-st** stocking/stockinette stitch;
tog together; **WS** wrong side; **yrn (yarn
round needle)** wrap yarn around right
needle from front to back and to front again
between needles to make a st

back

With 3¼mm(US 5) needles and M, cast on 63(69:75:81) sts.

Moss/seed st row K1 [p1, k1] to end.

This last row forms moss/seed st and is repeated.

Work in 3cm/1¼in in moss/seed st.

Beg with a RS (k) row, work in st-st until back measures 16(18:20:21)cm/6¼(7:7¾:8¼)in from cast-on edge, ending with a WS (p) row.

shape armholes

Cast/bind off 3(4:5:6) sts at beg of next 2 rows. 57(61:65:69) sts.

Dec 1 st at each end of next and 3(4:4:5) foll RS rows. 49(51:55:57) sts.

Cont straight until Back measures 30(33:36:38)cm/ 11¾(13:14:15)in from cast-on edge, ending with a WS row.

shape shoulders

Cast/bind off 8 sts at beg of next 4 rows.

Leave rem 17(19:23:25) sts on a holder.

pocket lining (make 1)

With 3¼mm(US 5) needles and M, cast on 15(17:19:21) sts.

Work 5(6:6:7)cm/2(2½:2½:2¾)in in st-st, ending with a WS row.

Leave sts on a holder.

left front

With 3¼mm(US 5) needles and M, cast on 35(37:41:43) sts.

Work 3cm/1¼in in moss/seed st as for Back.

Next row (RS) K to last 5 sts, moss/seed st 5.

Next row (WS) Moss/seed st 5, p to end.

These last 2 rows set the position for the st-st with moss/seed st button band and are repeated.

Work in patt as set until Front measures 8(8:10:10)cm/ 3¼(3¼:4:4)in from cast-on edge, ending with a WS row.

place pocket

Next row (RS) K10(10:12:12), slip next 15(17:19:21) sts onto a holder for pocket top, k across 15(17:19:21) sts of pocket lining, k5, moss/seed st 5.

Cont in patt as set, work until Front measures

16(18:20:21)cm/6¼(7:7¾:8¼)in from cast-on edge, ending with a WS row.

shape armhole

Cast/bind off 3(4:5:6) sts at beg of next row.

Work 1 row in patt.

Cont in patt, dec 1 st at armhole edge on next and 3(4:4:5) foll RS rows. 28(28:31:31) sts.

Cont straight in patt until Front measures 24(27:30:32)cm/ 9¼(10½:11¾:12½)in from cast-on edge, ending with a WS row.

shape neck

Next row (RS) K to last 5 sts and slip these rem 5 moss/seed sts at front edge onto a safety pin for neckband.

Cont in st-st, cast/bind off 2 sts at beg (neck edge) of next and foll 1(1:2:2) alt row(s), then dec 1 st at beg of foll 3(3:4:4) alt rows. 16 sts.

Cont straight until Front measures same as Back to shoulder, ending with a WS row.

shape shoulder

Cast/bind off 8 sts at beg of next row and foll alt row.

Mark the position for 5(6:6:7) buttons on the button band, the first on the 3rd moss/seed st row after cast-on, the last to come in the neckband and the rem 3(4:4:5) spaced evenly between.

right front

With 3¼mm(US 5) needles and M, cast on 35(37:41:43) sts.

Work 2 rows in moss/seed st as for Back.

Work first buttonhole on next row to match position of first button marker as foll:

Buttonhole row (RS) K1, p2tog, yrn, [p1, k1] to end.

Cont in moss/seed st until Front measures 3cm/1¼in from cast-on edge.

Next row (RS) Moss/seed st 5, k to end.

Next row (WS) P to last 5 sts, moss/seed st 5.

These last 2 rows set the position for the st-st with moss/seed st buttonhole band and are repeated.

Working buttonholes as before to match markers throughout and cont in patt as set, work until Front measures 16(18:20:21)cm/6¼(7:7¾:8¼)in from cast-on edge, ending with a RS row.

shape armhole

Cast/bind off 3(4:5:6) sts at beg of next row.

Cont in patt, dec 1 st at armhole edge on next and 3(4:4:5) foll RS rows. 28(28:31:31) sts.

Cont straight in patt until Front measures 24(27:30:32)cm/ 9¼(10½:11¾:12½)in from cast-on edge, ending with a RS row.

shape neck

Next row (WS) P to last 5 sts and slip these rem 5 moss/seed sts onto a safety pin for neckband.

Cont in st-st, cast/bind off 2 sts at beg (neck edge) of next and foll 1(1:2:2) alt row(s), then dec 1 st at beg of foll 3(3:4:4) alt rows. 16 sts.

Cont straight until Front measures same as Back to shoulder, ending with a RS row.

shape shoulder

Cast/bind off 8 sts at beg of next row and foll alt row.

sleeves

With 3¾mm(US 5) needles and M, cast on 33(35:37:39) sts.

Work 3cm/1¼in in moss/seed st as for Back.

Inc row (RS) K and inc 6 sts evenly across row. 39(41:43:45) sts.

Beg with a WS (p) row and working in st-st, inc 1 st at each end of 3rd and every foll 3rd row until there are 63(67:73:81) sts. Cont straight in st-st until Sleeve measures 18(21:23:28)cm/ 7(8¼:9:11)in from beg, ending with a WS row.

shape top

Cast/bind off 3(4:5:6) sts at beg of next 2 rows.

Dec 1 st at each end of next and 3(4:4:5) foll RS rows.

Cast/bind off rem 49(49:53:57) sts.

neckband

Join shoulder seams.

With WS facing, 3¾mm(US 5) needles and M, moss/seed st across 5 sts of right front band, turn and now with RS facing, moss/seed st 5, pick up and k 17 sts up right front neck, k across 17(19:23:25) sts from back neck holder, pick up and k 17 sts down left front neck, then moss/seed st across 5 sts of left front band. 61(63:67:69) sts.

Work 1 row in moss/seed st.

Buttonhole row (RS) K1, p2tog, yrn, moss/seed st to end.

Work 4 rows more in moss/seed st.

Cast/bind off in moss/seed st.

pocket tops

With RS facing, 3¾mm(US 5) needles and M, work 4 rows in moss/seed st across 15(17:19:21) sts on pocket top holder.

Cast/bind off in moss/seed st.

bobbles

Make several in each of six contrasting colours (A, B, C, D, E and F) as foll:

With 3¾mm(US 5) needles, cast on 1 st.

1st row (RS) [K1, p1, k1, p1, k1] all into 1 st. 5 sts.

Beg with a p row, work 3 rows in st-st on these 5 sts.

5th row (RS) Pass 2nd, 3rd, 4th and 5th sts over first st, then k into back of rem st.

Break yarn and pull through last st. Tie the two yarn ends together to create the bobble.

to finish

Sew sleeves into armholes. Join side and sleeve seams. Sew on buttons. Mixing the colours, sew bobbles to the back, fronts and sleeves above the moss/seed-st edges, and around the neck edge below moss/seed-st edge.

zip-up jacket

With it's chunky zip fastener and useful pockets, this multi-purpose jacket is ideal for playing outdoors and keeping found treasures safe.

materials

6(7:7:8) 50g/1¾oz balls of Debbie Bliss *Merino Aran* in red/Red 700

Pair of 5mm(US 8) knitting needles

25(25:30:30)/10(10:12:12)in open-ended zip fastener

6 small wooden buttons

sizes

to fit

6–12 mths	1–2	2–3	3–4	yrs
actual measurements				
chest				
56	61	66	71	cm
22	24	26	28	in
length				
30	33	36	38	cm
11¾	13	14	15	in
sleeve seam (with cuff turned back)				
18	21	23	28	cm
7	8¼	9	11	in

tension/gauge

18 sts and 32 rows to 10cm/4in over moss/seed stitch using 5mm(US 8) needles

abbreviations

beg beginning; **cm** centimetre(s); **cont** continu(e)(ing); **dec** decrease; **foll** follow(s)(ing); **in** inch(es); **inc** increase; **k** knit; **p** purl; **patt** pattern; **rem** remaining; **RS** right side; **st(s)** stitch(es); **st-st** stocking/stockinette stitch; **tbl** through back of loop(s); **tog** together; **WS** wrong side; **yo (yarn over needle)** take yarn over right needle to make a st; **yrn (yarn round needle)** wrap yarn around right needle from front to back and to front again between needles to make a st

back

With 5mm(US 8) needles, cast on 51(55:59:65) sts.
Moss/seed stitch row K1, [p1, k1] to end.
This last row forms moss/seed st and is repeated.
Working in moss/seed st throughout, cont until Back
measures 18(20:22:23)cm/7(8:8¼:9)in from cast-on edge,
ending with a WS row.

shape armholes

Cast/bind off 4(4:6:6) sts at beg of next 2 rows.
Cont straight until Back measures 30(33:36:38)cm/
11¼(13:14:15)in from cast-on edge, ending with a WS row.

shape shoulders

Cast/bind off 11(12:11:13) sts at beg of next 2 rows.
Leave rem 21(23:25:27) sts on a holder.

front pocket linings (make 2)

With 5mm(US 8) needles, cast on 11(13:13:15) sts.
Work 25(25:27:27) rows in moss/seed st.
Leave sts on a holder.

front pocket flaps (make 2)

With 5mm(US 8) needles, cast on 13(15:15:17) sts.
Work 2 rows in moss/seed st.
Buttonhole row K1, p1, k2tog, [yrn] twice, p2tog, k1,
[p1, k1] 0(1:1:2) times, p2tog, yrn, yo, k2tog, p1, k1.
Next row [K1, p1] twice, k1tbl, [p1, k1] 2(3:3:4) times,
p1tbl, k1, p1, k1.
Work 1 row in moss/seed st.
Leave sts on a holder.

left front

With 5mm(US 8) needles, cast on 23(25:29:31) sts.
Working in moss/seed st throughout, work until Front
measures 9(9:11:11)cm/3½(3½:4¼:4¼)in from cast-on edge,
ending with a WS row.

place pocket

Next row (RS) Moss/seed st 6(6:8:8), cast/bind off next
11(13:13:15) sts, moss/seed st to end.
Next row (WS) Moss/seed st 6(6:8:8), moss/seed st across
11(13:13:15) sts of one pocket lining, moss/seed st to end.

Next row (RS) Moss/seed st 5(5:7:7), holding pocket flap stitch holder at front of work, work pocket flap sts tog with next 13(15:15:17) sts of front, moss/seed st to end.

Cont straight until Front measures same as Back to armhole, ending with a WS row (a RS row for Right Front).

shape armhole

Cast/bind off 4(4:6:6) sts at beg of next row.

Cont straight until Front measures 25(27:30:31)cm/9¾(10½:11¾:12¼)in from cast-on edge, ending with a WS row (a RS row for Right Front).

shape neck

Next row Moss/seed st to last 3(4:5:5) sts and slip these rem 3(4:5:5) sts at Front edge onto a safety pin.

Work 2 rows in moss/seed st.

Cast/bind off 2 sts at beg (neck edge) of next row and 1 st at beg of foll 3(3:5:5) alt rows.

Work straight on rem 11(12:11:13) sts until Front matches Back to shoulder, ending with a WS row (a RS row for Right Front).

Cast/bind off in moss/seed st.

right front

Work as for Left Front, but noting exceptions in ( )s.

sleeve pocket lining (make 1)

With 5mm(US 8) needles, cast on 11 sts.

Work 17 rows in moss/seed st.

Leave sts on a holder.

sleeve pocket flap

With 5mm(US 8) needles, cast on 13 sts.

Work 2 rows in moss/seed st.

Buttonhole row K1, p1, k2tog, [yrn] twice, p2tog, k1, p2tog, yrn, yo, k2tog, p1, k1.

Next row [K1, p1] twice, k1tbl, [p1, k1] twice, p1tbl, k1, p1, k1.

Work 1 row in moss/seed st.

Leave sts on a holder.

left sleeve

With 5mm(US 8) needles, cast on 23(25:29:31) sts.

Work 26 rows in moss/seed st.

Cont in moss/seed st throughout, inc 1 st at each end of next and every foll 4th(4th:5th:6th) row, until there are 43(47:51:55) sts, taking inc sts into moss/seed st, **and at the same time** when Sleeve measures 16(19:21:26)cm/6¼(7½:8¼:10¼)in from cast-on edge, place the pocket lining and flap centrally over the next 3 rows as for Fronts.

When all sts have been increased, cont straight until Sleeve measures 22(25:27:32)cm/8½(9¾:10½:12½)in from cast-on edge.

Mark each end of last row, then work 7(7:10:10) rows more.

Cast/bind off.

right sleeve

Work as for Left Sleeve, but omitting pocket.

collar

Join shoulder seams.

With WS facing and 5mm(US 8) needles, moss/seed st across 3(4:5:5) sts on Right Front safety pin, turn, moss/seed st 3(4:5:5), pick up and k 15(17:17:20) sts up Right Front neck, moss/seed st across 21(23:25:27) sts on back neck holder, pick up and k 15(17:17:20) sts down Left Front neck, then moss/seed st across 3(4:5:5) sts on Left Front safety pin. 57(65:69:77) sts.

Work 15(15:17:17) rows in moss/seed st.

Cast/bind off.

to finish

Sew sleeves into armholes, joining row ends above markers to cast-/bound-off sts at underarm. Join sleeve seams. Join side seams, leaving lower 4cm/1½in open for side slits. Handstitch zip fastener to front edges. Slipstitch pocket linings in place. Sew buttons to pocket fronts to correspond with buttonholes.

robin hood jacket

This snuggly hooded jacket is perfect for keeping warm on cold autumn days. It is finished with wooden toggles and a cute tasseled hood.

materials

5(6:6:7) 50g/1¾oz balls of Rowan *Cork* in orange/Delight 040 or grey/Turbid 33
Pair each of 7mm(US 10½) and 7½mm(US 11) knitting needles
Cable needle
4 buttons or toggles

sizes

to fit

6–12 mths	1–2	2–3	3–4	yrs

actual measurements

chest

58	63	68	71	cm
23	25	27	28	in

length

30	33	36	38	cm
11¼	13	14	15	in

sleeve seam

18	21	23	27	cm
7	8¼	9	10¼	in

tension/gauge

16 sts and 23 rows to 10cm/4in over moss/seed st using 7½mm(US 11) needles

abbreviations

C4B (cable 4 back) sl next 2 sts onto cable needle and hold at back of work, k2, then k2 from cable needle; **C4F (cable 4 front)** as C4B, but hold cable needle in front of work; **cm** centimetre(s); **cont** continu(e)(ing); **Cr4L (cross 4 left)** sl next 2 sts onto cable needle and hold at front of work, p2, then k 2 from cable needle; **Cr4R (cross 4 right)** sl next 2 sts onto cable needle and hold at back of work, k2, then p2 from cable needle; **dec** decrease; **foll** follow(s)(ing); **in** inch(es); **inc** increas(e)(ing); **k** knit; **m1** make one st by picking up and working into back of loop lying between last st and next st; **p** purl; **patt** pattern; **rem** remaining; **rep** repeat; **RS** right side; **sl** slip; **st(s)** stitch(es); **tog** together; **WS** wrong side; **yrn (yarn round needle)** wrap yarn around right needle from front to back and to front again between needles to make a st

cable panel

Worked over a panel of 16 sts.

1st row (WS) P2, k4, p4, k4, p2.

2nd row (RS) K2, p4, C4F, p4, k2.

3rd and every foll WS row K all the k sts and p all p sts as they appear.

4th row Cr4L, p2, k4, p2, Cr4R.

6th row P2, Cr4L, C4F, Cr4R, p2.

8th row P4, C4B, C4B, p4.

10th row P2, Cr4R, C4F, Cr4L, p2.

12th row Cr4R, p2, k4, p2, Cr4L.

These 12 rows form the cable panel and are repeated in positions given in the instructions.

back

With 7mm(US 10½) needles, cast on 46(50:54:58) sts.

1st moss/seed st row (RS) [K1, p1] to end.

2nd moss/seed st row [P1, k1] to end.

Rep last 2 rows once more and first row again.

Inc row (WS) Moss/seed 2(4:2:4), m1, [moss/seed 2, m1] 1(1:3:3) times, moss/seed 3, m1, moss/seed 4, m1, moss/seed 2, m1, moss/seed 4, m1, moss/seed 3, [m1, moss/seed 2] 3 times, m1, moss/seed 3, m1, moss/seed 4, m1, moss/seed 2, m1, moss/seed 4, m1, moss/seed 3, [m1, moss/seed 2] 2(2:4:4) times, moss/seed 0(2:0:2). 62(66:74:78) sts.

Change to 7½mm(US 11) needles.

Foundation row (RS) P2(4:2:4), [k4, p2] 1(1:2:2) times, k2, p4, k4, p4, k2, p2, [k4, p2] twice, k2, p4, k4, p4, k2, [p2, k4] 1(1:2:2) times, p2(4:2:4).

1st row (WS) K2(4:2:4), [p4, k2] 1(1:2:2) times, work across 16 sts of first row of cable panel, k2, [p4, k2] twice, work across 16 sts of first row of cable panel, [k2, p4] 1(1:2:2) times, k2(4:2:4).

2nd row (RS) P2(4:2:4), [C4F, p2] 1(1:2:2) times, work 2nd row of cable panel, p2, [C4F, p2] twice, work 2nd row of cable panel, [p2, C4F] 1(1:2:2) times, p2(4:2:4).

3rd and every foll WS row K all the k sts and p all p sts as they appear.

4th row (RS) P2(4:2:4), [k4, p2] 1(1:2:2) times, work 4th row of cable panel, p2, [k4, p2] twice, work 4th row of cable panel, [p2, k4] 1(1:2:2) times, p2(4:2:4).

These last 4 rows set the position of the cable panels and form the simple 4-st cables and are repeated, working the correct cable panel rows.

Work in patt until Back measures 30(33:36:38)cm/11¾(13:14:15)in from cast-on edge, ending with a RS row and noting the cable panel row.

Cast/bind off all sts, working 2 sts tog in centre of each cable.

left front

With 7mm(US 10½) needles, cast on 27(29:31:33) sts.

Moss/seed st row K1, [p1, k1] to end.

Rep last row 4 more times.

Inc row (WS) Moss/seed 5, m1, moss/seed 2, m1, moss/seed 3, m1, moss/seed 4, m1, moss/seed 2, m1, moss/seed 4, m1, moss/seed 3, m1, [moss/seed 2, m1] 1(1:3:3) times, moss/seed 2(4:2:4). 35(37:41:43) sts.

Change to 7½mm(US 11) needles.

Foundation row (RS) P2(4:2:4), [k4, p2] 1(1:2:2) times, k2, p4, k4, p4, k2, p2, k4, p1, [p1, k1] twice.

1st row (WS) [k1, p1] twice, k1, p4, k2, work across 16 sts of first row of cable panel, [k2, p4] 1(1:2:2) times, k2(4:2:4).

2nd row (RS) P2(4:2:4), [C4F, p2] 1(1:2:2) times, work 2nd row of cable panel, p2, C4F, p1, [p1, k1] twice.

3rd row [k1, p1] twice, k1, p4, k2, work 3rd row of cable panel, [k2, p4] 1(1:2:2) times, k2(4:2:4).

4th row P2(4:2:4), [k4, p2] 1(1:2:2) times, work 4th row of cable panel, p2, k4, p1, [p1, k1] twice.

These last 4 rows set the position of the cable panel with moss/seed-st front border and form the simple 4-st cables and are repeated, working the correct cable panel rows.

Work in patt, ending 9 rows below Back, so ending with a WS row.

shape neck

Next row (RS) Patt to last 10 sts, turn, leave these 10 sts on a holder for hood and cont on rem 25(27:31:33) sts.

Dec 1 st at neck edge on next 7 rows.

Work 1 row.

Cast/bind off all sts, working 2 sts tog in centre of each cable.

Mark the position for 4 buttons on the front border, the first to be worked on the 3rd row after cast-on, the last just below neck shaping and the rem 2 spaced evenly between.

right front

With 7mm(US 10½) needles, cast on 27(29:31:33) sts.

Moss/seed st row K1, [p1, k1] to end.

Rep last row once more.

Buttonhole row (RS) K1, p1, yrn, p2tog, k1, [p1, k1] to end.

Work 2 rows in moss/seed st.

Inc row (WS) Moss/seed 2(4:2:4), m1, [moss/seed 2, m1] 1(1:3:3) times, moss/seed 3, m1, moss/seed 4, m1, moss/seed 2, m1, moss/seed 4, m1, moss/seed 3, m1, moss/seed 2, m1, moss/seed 5.

Change to 7½mm(US 11) needles.

Foundation row (RS) [K1, p1] twice, p1, k4, p2, k2, p4, k4, p4, k2, [p2, k4] 1(1:2:2) times, p2(4:2:4).

1st row (WS) K2(4:2:4), [p4, k2] 1(1:2:2) times, work 16 sts of first row of cable panel, k2, p4, k1, [p1, k1] twice.

2nd row (RS) [K1, p1] twice, p1, C4F, p2, work 2nd

row of cable panel, [p2, C4F] 1(1:2:2) times, p2(4:2:4).

3rd row K2(4:2:4), [p4, k2] 1(1:2:2) times, work 3rd row of cable panel, k2, p4, k1, [p1, k1] twice.

4th row [K1, p1] twice, p1, k4, p2, work 4th row of cable panel, [p2, k4] 1(1:2:2) times, p2(4:2:4).

These last 4 rows set the position of the cable panel with moss/seed-st front border and form the simple 4-st cables and are repeated, working the correct cable panel rows.

Working buttonholes as before on RS rows to match markers, work in patt, ending 9 rows below Back, so ending with a WS row.

shape neck

Next row (RS) Patt 10 sts and slip these onto a holder for hood, patt to end.

Dec 1 st at neck edge on next 7 rows.

Work 1 row.

Cast/bind off all sts, working 2 sts tog in centre of each cable.

sleeves

With 7mm(US 10½) needles, cast on 22(22:26:26) sts.

1st moss/seed st row (RS) [K1, p1] to end.

2nd moss/seed st row [P1, k1] to end.

Rep last 2 rows once more and first row again.

Inc row (WS) Work in moss/seed st and inc 10(10:12:12) sts evenly across row. 32(32:38:38) sts.

Change to 7½mm(US 11) needles.

Foundation row (RS) Moss/seed st 1(1:4:4) sts, p1, k4, p2, k2, p4, k4, p4, k2, p2, k4, p1, moss/seed st 1(1:4:4) sts.

1st row (WS) Moss/seed st 1(1:4:4) sts, k1, p4, k2, work across 16 sts of first row of cable panel, k2, p4, k1, moss/seed st 1(1:4:4) sts.

2nd row (RS) Moss/seed st 1(1:4:4) sts, p1, C4F, p2, work 2nd row of cable panel, p2, C4F, p1, moss/seed st 1(1:4:4) sts.

3rd row Moss/seed st 1(1:4:4) sts, k1, p4, k2, work 3rd row of cable panel, k2, p4, k1, moss/seed st 1(1:4:4) sts.

4th row Moss/seed st 1(1:4:4) sts, p1, k4, p2, work 4th row of cable panel, p2, k4, p1, moss/seed st 1(1:4:4) sts.

These last 4 rows set the position of the cable panel and 4-st cables with moss/seed st to each side and are repeated, working correct cable panel rows.

Working in patt as set, inc 1 st at each end of next RS row and every foll 6th row until there are 42(44:50:52) sts, taking inc sts into moss/seed st.

Cont straight in patt until Sleeve measures 18(21:23:27)cm/7(8¼:9:10¾)in from cast-on edge, ending with a RS row.

Cast/bind off, working 2 sts tog in centre of each cable.

hood

Join shoulder seams.

With RS facing and 7mm(US 10½) needles, slip 10 sts from right front holder onto needle, pick up and k 10 sts up right front neck, 27 sts across back neck, and 10 sts down left front neck, then patt across 10 sts on left front holder. 67 sts.

1st row (WS) [K1, p1] twice, k1, p4, k1, [p1, k1] 5 times, moss/seed across 27 sts of back neck and inc 8 sts evenly, [k1, p1] 5 times, k1, p4, k1, [p1, k1] twice.

This last row sets the position of the moss/seed and cable border with moss/seed st between.

Cont straight in patt as set, keeping the cables correct until hood measures 21(24:27:29)cm/8¼(9½:10¾:11½)in from cast-on edge.

Cast/bind off.

to finish

Fold cast/bound-off edge of hood in half and join seam. Matching centre of cast/bound-off edge of sleeve to shoulder seam, sew on sleeves. Join side and sleeve seams. Sew on buttons. Make a tassel and sew to hood point.

hearts & stars blanket

This blanket is great for family picnics or just keeping on the sofa for cold evenings. It looks great in almost any colour, so why not knit it in your own favourite?

materials

14 50g/1¾oz balls of Rowan *Handknit DK Cotton* in orange/Flame 254
Pair of extra-long 4mm(US 6) knitting needles

size

Approximately 83cm/32¼in by 110cm/43¼in

tension/gauge

20 sts and 28 rows to 10cm/4in over st-st using 4mm(US 6) needles

abbreviations

cm centimetre(s); **in** inch(es); **k** knit; **p** purl; **rep** repeat; **RS** right side; **st(s)** stitch(es); **st-st** stocking/stockinette stitch; **WS** wrong side

note

The blanket can also be worked back and forth in rows (not in rounds) with a long circular needle.

to make

With 4mm(US 6) needles, cast on 167 sts.

Moss/seed st row K1, [p1, k1] to end.

Rep this row 9 times more.

place charts

***Next row (RS)** *K1, [p1, k1] 3 times, work across
25 sts of first row of star chart, k1, [p1, k1] 3 times,
work across 25 sts of first row of heart chart; rep from
* once more, k1, [p1, k1] 3 times, work across 25 sts of
first row of star chart, k1, [p1, k1] 3 times.

This row sets the position of the first line of charts with
7 moss/seed sts between each chart and at each side
edge.

Work as set until all 36 chart rows have been completed.

Work 10 moss/seed st rows as set, so ending with a WS
row.**

Next row (RS) *K1, [p1, k1] 3 times, work across 25
sts of first row of heart chart, k1, [p1, k1] 3 times,
work across 25 sts of first row of star chart; rep from *
once more, k1, [p1, k1] 3 times, work across 25 sts of
first row of heart chart, k1, [p1, k1] 3 times.

This row sets the position of the second line of charts
with 7 moss/seed sts between each chart and at
each side edge.

Work as set until all 36 chart rows have been completed.

Work 10 moss/seed st rows as set, so ending with a WS
row.***

Rep the 92 rows from *** to *** twice more and then
rep the 46 rows from *** to ** once more.

Cast/bind off in moss/seed st.

key

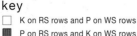

☐ K on RS rows and P on WS rows

■ P on RS rows and K on WS rows

star chart

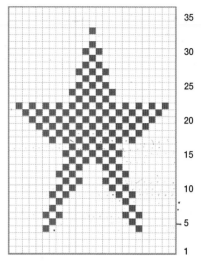

35
30
25
20
15
10
5
1

heart chart

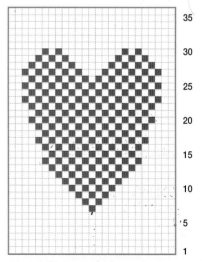

35
30
25
20
15
10
5
1

heads, toes & little hands

fair isle tassel hat

This cute hat with fun tassels will keep little heads warm and cosy. The bright Fair Isle design will brighten up even the darkest winter day.

materials

One 50g/1¾oz ball each of King Cole *Anti-Tickle Merino DK* in **A** (hot pink/Raspberry 67), **B** (baby pink/Dusky Pink 94), **C** (blue/Bluebell 26), **D** (light blue/Sky 5) and **E** (cream/Aran 46)

Pair of size 3¼mm(US 3) and 4mm(US 6) knitting needles

sizes

to fit

6–12 mths	1–2	2–3	3–4	yrs

tension/gauge

25 sts and 26 rows to 10cm/4in over patterned st-st using 4mm(US 6) needles

abbreviations

beg beginning; **cm** centimetre(s); **in** inch(es); **k** knit; **p** purl; **RS** right side; **st(s)** stitch(es); **st-st** stocking/stockinette stitch; **WS** wrong side

HEADS, TOES & LITTLE HANDS

to make

With 3¼mm(US 3) needles and A, cast on 45(53:57:61) sts.

Moss/seed st row K1, [p1, k1] to end.

This row forms moss/seed st and is repeated.

Work 7(7:8:8)cm/2¾(2¾:3¼:3¼)in in moss/seed st.

Change to 4mm(US 6) needles.

Beg with a RS (k) row, work 10(11:12:13)cm/4(4¼:4¾:5)in in st-st from chart, ending with WS row and noting the chart row.

With A, k 3 rows.

Beg with the same noted WS (p) chart row, work 10(11:12:13)cm/4(4¼:4¾:5)in in st-st from chart, working back down the chart and ending with the first chart row.

Change to 3¼mm(US 3) needles and A.

P 1 row.

Work 7(7:8:8)cm/2¾(2¾:3¼:3¼)in in moss/seed st.

Cast/bind off.

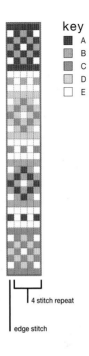

key

- A
- B
- C
- D
- E

4 stitch repeat

edge stitch

to finish

Fold the hat in half across the middle along the central ridge row, matching the cast-on and cast-/bound-off edge. Join the side seams.

Make 2 tassels in A, by winding yarn around your fingers about 24 times. Cut the yarn. Thread a short length through the loops and tie to hold the loops together. Wind another short length around the loops about 1cm/⅛in below the tied top and secure. Cut through the lower end of the loops, so making the tassel. Sew tassels to the top corners of the hat.

striped hat & scarf set

Little ones need to keep extra warm on cold days, so why not knit this trendy hat and scarf set to keep your child warm and looking great too?

materials

One 50g/1¾oz ball each of King Cole *Anti-Tickle Merino DK* in **A**, **B**, **C**, **D** and **E** (see *Note*)

Pair each of 3¼mm(US 3) and 3¾mm(US 5) knitting needles

Long 3¼mm(US 3) circular needle (for scarf only)

sizes

Hat

small   medium   large

Scarf

Approximately 92cm/36in by 16cm/6¼in

tension/gauge

23 sts and 32 rows to 10cm/4in over st-st using 3¾mm(US 5) needles

abbreviations

beg beginning; **cont** continu(e)(ing); **cm** centimetre(s); **foll** follow(s)(ing); **in** inch(es); **inc** increase; **k** knit; **p** purl; **patt** pattern; **rem** remaining; **rep** repeat; **RS** right side; **st(s)** stitch(es); **st-st** stocking/stockinette stitch; **tog** together; **WS** wrong side

note

Choose colours from the foll:
For **A**, turquoise/Turquoise 18 or yellow/Gold 55.
For **B**, cream/Aran 46.
For **C**, hot pink/Raspberry 67 or blue/Bluebell 26.
For **D**, baby pink/Dusky Pink 94 or turquoise/Turquoise 18.
For **E**, mauve/Larkspur 13 or light orange/Amber 10

earflap, cast on 32(36:44) sts, k across 17(19:21) sts of rem earflap, then cast on 12(14:17) sts. 90(102:120) sts. Beg with a WS (p) row and cont in st-st stripe patt as set, work 19(20:23) rows more.

2nd size only

Next row (WS) P2tog, p to last 2 sts, p2tog. 90(100:120) sts.

all sizes

K 1 row.

shape top

Shape top of hat as foll:

1st row (WS) [P2tog, p8] to end.

K 1 row, then p 1 row.

4th row (RS) [K7, k2tog] to end.

P 1 row, then k 1 row.

7th row (WS) [P2tog, p6] to end.

K 1 row, then p 1 row.

10th row (RS) [K5, k2tog] to end. 54(60:72) sts.

1st size only

11th row [P2tog, p4] to end. 45 sts.

12th row [K3, k2tog] to end. 36 sts.

13th row [P2tog, p2] to end. 27 sts.

14th row [K2tog, k1] to end. 18 sts.

15th row [P2tog] to end. 9 sts.

16th row [K2tog] 4 times, k1. 5 sts.

Break yarn, thread through rem 5 sts, pull up and secure.

2nd size only

P 1 row.

12th row (RS) [K4, k2tog] to end. 50 sts.

P 1 row.

14th row [K3, k2tog] to end. 40 sts.

P 1 row.

16th row [K2, k2tog] to end. 30 sts.

17th row [P1, p2tog] to end. 20 sts.

18th row [K2tog] to end. 10 sts.

P 1 row.

20th row [P2tog] to end. 5 sts.

earflaps for hat (make 2)

Using 3¼mm(US 5) needles and A, cast on 7(9:11) sts. Beg with a RS (k) row and working in 20-row st-st stripe repeat of 4 rows A, 4 rows B, 4 rows C, 4 rows D, 4 rows E, shape flaps as foll:

Inc 1 st at each end of first, 2nd, 4th, 5th, and 7th rows. 17(19:21) sts.

Work straight for 7(9:11) rows more.

Leave sts on a spare needle.

main hat

With RS of earflaps facing, 3¼mm(US 5) needles and colour to keep earflap stripe patt correct as set on earflaps, cast on 12(14:17) sts, k across 17(19:21) sts of one

Break yarn, thread through rem 5 sts, pull up and secure.

3rd size only

P 1 row.

12th row (RS) [K4, k2tog] to end. 60 sts.

P 1 row.

14th row [K3, k2tog] to end. 48 sts.

P 1 row.

16th row [K2, k2tog] to end. 36 sts.

P 1 row.

18th row [K1, k2tog] to end. 24 sts.

P 1 row.

20th row [K2tog] to end. 12 sts.

21st row [P2tog] to end. 6 sts.

22nd row [K2tog] to end. 3 sts.

Break yarn, thread through rem 3 sts, pull up and secure.

edging for hat

With RS facing, 3¼mm(US 3) needles and C, pick up and
k 12(14:17) sts across cast-on sts, 36(40:44) sts around
right earflap, 32(36:44) sts across front cast-on sts,
36(40:44) sts around left earflap and 12(14:17) sts across
cast-on sts. 128(144:166) sts.

K 2 rows.

Cast/bind off knitwise.

to finish hat

Join back seam. Cut six 60cm/24in lengths of C. Thread
three of the lengths through the centre of the edging of
each earflap. Taking three pairs of yarn lengths, make a
plait/braid, knot the ends and trim.

to make scarf

With 3¼mm(US 5) needles and B, cast on 33 sts.
Beg with a RS (k) row, work 20 rows in st-st stripe
sequence as foll:

4 rows B, 4 rows C, 4 rows D, 4 rows E and 4 rows A.
Rep last 20 rows 13 times more.

Cont in st-st, work 4 rows in B.

Change to long 3¼mm(US 3) circular needle and C.

Next row (RS) K33, pick up and k 284 sts along one
edge of scarf (1 st in each row), 33 sts across cast-on edge
and 284 sts along rem edge of scarf. 634 sts.

Working in rounds, p 1 round, k 1 round, then cast/bind
off purlwise on next round.

cabled hat with earflaps

Children will love this hat with its bunny-tail bobble on top. The ties will keep it firmly in place and the earflaps will make sure that little ears stay snug and warm.

materials

One 50g/1¾oz ball each of King Cole
   Anti-Tickle Merino DK in main colour **M**
   (turquoise/Turquoise 18; or hot pink/
   Raspberry 67) and contrasting colour
   A (blue/Bluebell 26; or cream/Aran 46)
Cable needle
Pair of 3¾mm(US 5) knitting needles
   3¼mm(US 3) circular needle

sizes

small   medium   large

tension/gauge

23 sts and 32 rows to 10cm/4in over st-st
using 3¾mm(US 5) needles

abbreviations

beg beginning; **cm** centimetre(s); **C6F**
(cable 6 front) sl next 3 sts onto cable
needle and hold at front, k3, then k3 from
cable needle; **in** inch(es); **k** knit; **kfb** k into
front and back of next st to inc 1 st; **p** purl;
patt pattern; **pfb** p into front and back of
next st to inc 1 st; **rem** remaining; **RS** right
side; **sl** slip; **skpo** sl 1, k1, pass slipped st
over; **sk2togpo** sl 1, k2tog, pass slipped st
over; **st(s)** stitch(es); **st-st** stocking/
stockinette stitch; **tog** together; **WS** wrong
side

earflaps (make 2)

With 3¾mm(US 5) needles and M, cast on 10 sts.

1st row (RS) Kfb, p1, k6, p1, kfb. 12 sts.

2nd row Pfb, p1, k1, p6, k1, p1, pfb. 14 sts.

3rd row K3, p1, k6, p1, k3.

4th row Pfb, p2, k1, p6, k1, p2, pfb. 16 sts.

5th row (cable crossing row) Kfb, k3, p1, C6F, p1, k3, kfb. 18 sts.

6th row P5, k1, p6, k1, p5.

7th row K5, p1, k6, p1, k5.

8th and 9th rows As 6th and 7th rows.

10th row As 6th row.

11th row (cable crossing row) K5, p1, C6F, p1, k5.

12th–15th rows Rep 6th and 7th rows twice.

These last 15 rows set the position of the cable which is crossed on every foll 6th row.

Leave sts on a holder.

main hat

With WS of earflaps facing, 3¾mm(US 5) needles and M, cast on 14(16:18) sts, work [p5, k1, p6, k1, p5] across one earflap, cast on 42(50:58) sts, work [p5, k1, p6, k1, p5] across rem earflap, cast on 14(16:18) sts. 106(118:130) sts.

Foundation row (RS) K4, p1, k6, p1, k7(9:11), p1, C6F, p1, [k7(9:11), p1, k6, p1] 3 times, k7(9:11), p1, C6F, p1, k7(9:11), p1, k6, p1, k4.

1st row P4, [k1, p6, k1, p7(9:11)] 6 times, k1, p6, k1, p4.

2nd row K4, [p1, k6, p1, k7(9:11)] 6 times, p1, k6, p1, k4.

3rd and 4th rows As first and 2nd rows.

5th row As first row.

6th row K4, [p1, C6F, p1, k7(9:11)] 6 times, p1, C6F, p1, k4.

These last 6 rows form the patt and are repeated.

Cont in patt until work measures 7.5cm/3in from cast-on edge, ending with a 5th row.

3rd size only

Next row (RS) K4, [p1, C6F, p1, skpo, k7, k2tog] 6 times, p1, C6F, p1, k4. 118 sts.

Patt 5 rows.

2nd and 3rd sizes only

Next row (RS) K4, [p1, C6F, p1, skpo, k5, k2tog] 6 times, p1, C6F, p1, k4. 106 sts.

Patt 5 rows.

all sizes

Next row (RS) K2, [k2tog, p1, C6F, p1, skpo, k3] 6 times, k2tog, p1, C6F, p1, skpo, k2. 92 sts.

Patt 3 rows.

Next row (RS) K1, [k2tog, p1, k6, p1, skpo, k1] 6 times, k2tog, p1, k6, p1, skpo, k1. 78 sts.

Patt 3 rows.

Next row (RS) K2, [p1, k6, p1, sk2togpo] 6 times, p1, k6, p1, k2. 66 sts.

Patt 1 row.

Next row (RS) K1, p2tog, [k6, p3tog] 6 times, k6, p2tog, k1. 52 sts.

Patt 1 row.

Next row (RS) K1, [p1, C6F] 7 times, p1, k1.

Next row P1, p2tog, [p1, p2tog, p1, p3tog] 6 times, [p1, p2tog] twice, p1. 31 sts.

Next row [K2tog, k2] 7 times, k2tog, k1. 23 sts.

Next row [P1, p2tog] 7 times, p2. 16 sts.

Next row K1, [k2tog] 7 times, k1. 9 sts.

Next row [P3tog] 3 times.

Break yarn leaving a 30cm/12in length for sewing up, thread through rem 3 sts, pull up and secure.

edging

With RS facing, 3¼mm(US 3) circular needle and A, pick up and k 13(15:17) sts across cast-on sts, 37 sts around right earflap, 42(50:58) sts across front cast-on sts, 37 sts around left earflap, and 13(15:17) sts across cast-on sts. 142(154:166) sts.

K 2 rows.

Cast/bind off knitwise.

to finish

Join back seam. Make a pompon from A and stitch to the top of the hat.

To make the ties, cut six 60cm/24in lengths of A. Thread three of the lengths through the centre of the edging of each earflap. Taking three pairs of yarn lengths, make a plait/braid, knot the ends and trim.

bold banded mittens

Mittens on strings are a great idea. Simply thread these striped mittens through your child's winter coat and the string will stop them from losing one.

materials

One 50g/1¾oz ball each of King Cole *Anti-Tickle Merino DK* in main colour **M** (red/Cherry 29 or cream/Aran 46) and **A** (cream/Aran 46; or blue/Bluebell 26)

Pair each of 3¼mm(US 3) and 3¾mm(US 5) knitting needles

sizes

to fit

| 3–6 mths | 1–2 | 3–4 | yrs |

tension/gauge

23 sts and 32 rows to 10cm/4in over st-st using 3¾mm(US 5) needles

abbreviations

alt alternate; **beg** beginning; **cm** centimetre(s); **cont** continu(e)(ing); **dec** decrease; **foll** follow(s)(ing); **in** inch(es); **inc** increas(e)(ing); **k** knit; **m1** make one stitch by picking up and working into back of loop lying between last st and next st; **p** purl; **patt** pattern; **rem** remaining; **rep** repeat; **RS** right side; **ssk** sl 1 knitwise, sl 1 knitwise, insert tip of left needle into fronts of 2 slipped sts and k2tog through back of loops; **tog** together; **WS** wrong side

note

Mittens for smallest size have no thumbs and are identical.

right mitten

With 3¼mm(US 3) needles and M, cast on 27(31:35) sts.

1st rib row (RS) K1, [p1, k1] to end.

2nd rib row P1, [k1, p1] to end.

These last 2 rows form rib patt and are repeated.

Work 3(3:4)cm/1¼(1¼:1½)in in rib, ending with a 2nd rib row and inc 1 st in centre of last row for 3rd size only. 27(31:36) sts.

Change to 3¾mm(US 5) needles and A.

1st size only

Beg with a RS (k) row and working in 4-row st-st stripe repeat of 2 rows A, 2 rows M, work 12 rows.

2nd and 3rd sizes only

Beg with a RS (k) row and working in 4-row st-st stripe repeat of 2 rows A, 2 rows M, work (0:2) rows.**

shape for thumb

Keeping st-st stripe patt (2 rows A, 2 rows M) correct, shape thumb as foll:

Inc row (RS) K(16:18), m1, k(1:2), m1, k(14:16).

P 1 row.

Inc row (RS) K(16:18), m1, k(3:4), m1, k(14:16).

P 1 row.

Inc row (RS) K(16:18), m1, k(5:6), m1, k(14:16).

P 1 row.

Cont in this way, inc 2 st as set on every alt row until there are (41:46) sts, ending with a WS (p) row.

Next row (RS) K(27:30), turn.

***Work in (M:A) only as foll:

Next row Cast on 1 st, p(12:13) including cast-on st, turn and cast on 1 st.

Work 8 rows in st-st on these (13:14) sts only.

Next row [K2tog] 3 times, k(1:0), [k2tog] (3:4) times. 7 sts. Break yarn, thread through 7 rem sts, pull up and secure. Join thumb seam.

With RS facing and keeping stripe patt correct, rejoin yarn to base of thumb, pick up and k (3:4) sts at base of thumb, then k rem sts. (33:38) sts.

Work 9 rows in stripe patt.

all sizes

Keeping stripe patt correct, shape top as foll:

Dec row K1, ssk, k8(11:13), k2tog, k1(1:2), ssk, k8(11:13),
k2tog, k1.

Work 3 rows.

Dec row K1, ssk, k6(9:11), k2tog, k1(1:2), ssk, k6(9:11),
k2tog, k1.

Work 1(1:3) rows.

Dec row K1, ssk, k4(7:9), k2tog, k1(1:2), ssk, k4(7:9),
k2tog, k1.

P 1 row.

Cast/bind off.

left mitten

1st size only

Work Left Mitten as for Right Mitten.

2nd and 3rd sizes only

Work as for Right Mitten to **.

shape for thumb

Keeping stripe patt (2 rows A, 2 rows M) correct, shape thumb as foll:

Inc row (RS) K(14:16), m1, k(1:2), m1, k(16:18)

P 1 row.

Inc row (RS) K(14:16), m1, k(3:4), m1, k(16:18).

P 1 row.

Inc row (RS) K(14:16), m1, k(5:6), m1, k(16:18).

P 1 row.

Cont in this way, inc 2 st as set on every alt row until there are (41:46) sts, ending with a WS (p) row.

Next row (RS) K(25:28), turn.

Complete as given for Right Mitten from *** to end.

to finish

Join seam. Make a 70(85:100)cm/27½(33½:39¼)in plait/braid as foll:

Cut three 2(2.5:3)m/2(2½:3)yd lengths of A, fold each length in half and tie the lengths together at folded end. Plait/braid the three doubled lengths into a single plait/braid and knot the end to secure. Stitch one end of the plait/braid to the seam inside the right mitten and the other end to the seam inside the left mitten. Thread the plait/braid through the sleeves of the child's coat, so one mitten hangs out of each sleeve end ready to wear.

polka dot bootees & hat

Knitted in luxuriously soft yarn, this hat and bootee set will make a stylish gift for a new baby.

materials

Bootees

One 50g/1¾oz ball each (see *Note*) of Debbie Bliss *Baby Cashmerino* in **A** (pale blue/Pale Blue 202; or beige/Stone 102; or pale pink/Pale Pink 600) and **B** (off-white/Ecru 101)

Pair of 3mm (US 2–3) knitting needles

Hat

One 50g/1¾oz ball each (see *Note*) of Debbie Bliss *Baby Cashmerino* in **A** (pale blue/Pale Blue 202;or beige/Stone 102; or pale pink/Pale Pink 600)and **B** (off-white/Ecru 101)

Pair of 3mm(US 2–3) knitting needles

sizes

Bootees

to fit

3–6 mths

Hat

to fit

3–6 mths   6–12 mths

tension/gauge

30 sts and 36 rows to 10cm/4in over patterned st-st using 3mm (US 2–3) needles

abbreviations

alt alternate; **cm** centimetre(s); **cont** continu(e)(ing); **dec** decrease; **in** inch(es); **foll** follow(s)(ing); **in** inch(es); **k** knit; **kfb** k into front and back of next st; **kp** knit then purl into next st; **m1** make one st by picking up and working into back of loop between last st and next st; **p** purl; **pfb** p into front and back of next st; **pk** purl then knit into next st; **rem** remaining; **rep** repeat; **RS** right side; **st(s)** stitch(es); **st-st** stocking/stockinette stitch; **tog** together; **WS** wrong side

note

Hat and bootees together can be made from one ball each in A and B.

to make bootees (makes 2)

Bootees are worked throughout on 3mm(US 2–3) needles and are worked in one piece starting at heel end of sole.

sole

With 3mm(US 2–3) needles and A, cast on 3 sts.

1st row (RS) K1, p1, k1.

2nd row Pk, pk, p1.

hat chart

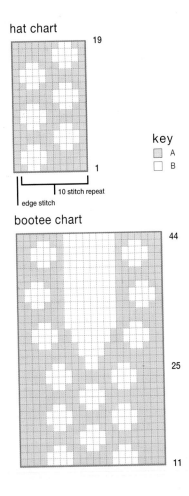

key

☐ A
☐ B

10 stitch repeat
edge stitch

bootee chart

3rd row Kp, k1, p1, kp, k1. 7 sts.

4th row [K1, p1] 3 times, k1.

5th row Pk, [p1, k1] twice, pk, p1.

6th row Kp, [k1, p1] 3 times, kp, k1.

7th row [K1, p1] 5 times, k1.

8th row Pk, [p1, k1] 4 times, pk, p1. 13 sts.

9th–36th rows [P1, k1] to last st, p1.

Dec 1 st at each end of next and 3 foll alt rows. 5 sts.

Next row (WS) P2, pfb, p2. 6 sts.

upper

Beg with a RS (k) row, work in st-st as foll:

1st row (RS) With A, kfb, k3, kfb, k1.

2nd row P in A.

3rd row With A, [kfb] twice, k3, [kfb] twice, k1. 12 sts.

4th row P in A.

5th row With A, [kfb] twice, k7, [kfb] twice, k1. 16 sts.

6th row P in A.

7th row KfbA, k6A, k2B, k5A, kfbA, k1A. 18 sts.

8th row P7A, p4B, p7A.

9th row K7A, k4B, k7A.

10th row [PfbA] twice, p1A, p2B, p3A, p2B, p3A, p2B, p2A, [pfbA] twice, p1A. 22 sts.

11th–24th rows Work in patterned st-st from bootee chart.

25th row Cont to work from chart, k5A, k2B, k3A, turn and cont on these sts only, leaving rem sts on a spare needle.

26th–44th rows Cont in st-st from chart **and at the same time** dec 1 st at ankle edge on 3 foll alt rows as indicated.

Cast/bind off.

With RS facing, slip 2 sts at centre front onto a safety pin, rejoin yarn to rem sts and complete chart.

cuff

With RS facing, 3mm(US 2–3) needles and A, pick up and k 19 sts down ankle edge to centre front, [k1, m1, k1] from sts on safety pin, then pick up and k 19 sts up ankle edge. 41 sts.

1st rib row (WS) P1, [k1, p1] to end.

2nd rib row (RS) K1, [p1, k1] to end.

Rep last 2 rows 12 more times.

Change to B.

Next row (WS) K.

Cast/bind off.

to make hat

With 3mm(US 2–3) needles and B, cast on 111(121) sts.

Change to A and k 1 row.

1st rib row K1, [p1, k1] to end.

2nd rib row P1, [k1, p1] to end.

Rep last 2 rows until cuff measures 6.5(8)cm/2¼(3¼)in from cast-on edge, ending with a 2nd rib row and dec 1 st in centre for 1st size only. 110(121) sts.

Beg with a RS (k) row work 2 rows. Now work 19 rows in st-st from hat chart and inc 1 st at end of last row for 1st size only. Cont in A only.

22nd row (WS) P1, [p2tog, p8] 11(12) times. 100 (109) sts.

Cont in st-st in A only, work 2 rows.

Next row (RS) [K7, k2tog] 11(12) times, k1. 89(97) sts.

Work 3 rows.

Next row [K6, k2tog] 11(12) times, k1. 78(85) sts.

Work 3 rows.

Next row [K5, k2tog] 11(12) times, k1. 67(73) sts.

Work 1(3) rows.

Next row [K4, k2tog] 11(12) times, k1. 56(61) sts.

Work 1(3) rows.

Cont to dec 11(12) sts as set on every foll RS row until 23(25) sts rem. P 1 row.

Next row [K2tog] 11(12) times, k1. 12(13) sts.

Next row P0(1), [p2tog] 6 times. 6(7) sts.

Break yarn leaving a long end for sewing seam, thread through rem 6(7) sts, pull up and secure.

to finish

Join back seam, reversing lower part of ribbed cuff seam to allow for turn back. Make a pompon using B and sew to top of hat.

baby slippers

Who could resist these tiny shoes? They are easy to make
and finished with simple cross stitch embroidery and stylish
mother-of-pearl buttons.

materials

One 50g/1¾oz ball of Rowan *Cotton
   Glacé* in main colour **M**
   (red/Poppy 741) and small
   amount in **A** (off-white/Ecru 725)
Pair of 2¾mm(US 2) knitting needles
2 small buttons

sizes

to fit
3–6   6–12   mths

tension/gauge

28 sts and 44 rows to 10cm/4in over
moss/seed st using 2¾mm(US 2)
needles

abbreviations

alt alternate; **cm** centimetre(s);
cont continu(e)(ing); **dec** decrease;
foll follow(s)(ing); **in** inch(es);
inc increase; **k** knit; **p** purl;
st(s) stitch(es); **tog** together

note

Moss/seed st is reversible, so take care when you
sew together the second slipper that it is a mirror
image of the first.

slippers (makes 2)

Each slipper is made in one piece.

sole

With 2¼mm(US 2) needles and M, cast on 20(24) sts.
Beg moss/seed st sole as foll:

1st row [K1, p1] to end.

2nd row Cast on 1 st, [p1, k1] to end, cast on 1 st.
22(26) sts.

3rd row [P1, k1] to end.

Cont in moss/seed st as set and taking inc sts into
moss/seed st, inc 1 st at each end of next and 2 foll alt
rows. 28(32) sts.

Keeping moss/seed st correct as set throughout, work 3
rows.

Dec 1 st at each end of next and 3 foll alt rows. 20(24) sts.

19th row Moss/seed st to end, cast on 7(8) sts. 27(32) sts

upper

1st row Work in moss/seed st.

Inc 1 st at beg of next and every foll alt row until there
are 32(38) sts.

11th(13th) row Cast/bind off 12 sts, moss/seed st 5,
cast/bind off 4(5) sts, moss/seed st to end.

12th(14th) row Moss/seed st 11(16), leave 5 sts on a
safety pin for strap.

13th(15th)–21st(25th) rows Work in moss/seed st.

22nd(26th) row Moss/seed st 11(16), cast on 21(22)
sts.

23rd(27th) row Work in moss/seed st.

Dec 1 st at beg of next and 4(5) foll alt rows.

Cast/bind off rem 27(32) sts.

strap

Slip 5 sts from safety pin onto a needle.

With 2¼mm(US 2) needles, work 21 rows in
moss/seed st as set.

Buttonhole row Moss/seed st 2, make *yarn-over* for
buttonhole by wrapping yarn around right needle,
work 2tog, moss/seed st 1.

Work 1 row in moss/seed st.

Next row Work 2tog, moss/seed st 1, work 2tog.
Cast/bind off rem 3 sts.

to finish

Join heel seam. Carefully stitch upper to sole, easing in
fullness at toe. Sew one button to each slipper. Work
cross stitches around edge in A.

useful information

knitting abbreviations

The following are the general abbreviations used in the knitting patterns. Special abbreviations, such as those for cable patterns, are given with the individual patterns.

alt alternate

beg begin(ning)

cm centimetre(s)

cont continu(e)(ing)

cont straight continu(e)(ing) without shaping

dec decreas(e)(ing)

foll follow(s)(ing)

g gram(s)

in inch(es)

inc increas(e)(ing)

k knit

kfb k into front and back of next st to inc one st

kp knit then purl into next st

m metre(s)

m1 make one st by picking up and working into back of loop between last st and next st

mm millimetre(s)

oz ounce(s)

p purl

patt pattern

pfb p into front and back of next st to inc one st

pk purl then knit into next st

psso pass slipped stitch over

rem remain(s)(ing)

rep repeat(s)(ing)

RS right side

skpo slip 1, k1, pass slipped st over

sk2togpo slip 1, k2tog, pass slipped st over

sl slip

ssk slip 1 knitwise, slip 1 knitwise, insert tip of left needle into fronts of 2 slipped sts and k2tog tbl

st(s) stitch(es)

st-st stocking/stockinette stitch

tbl through back of loop(s)

tog together

WS wrong side

yd yard(s)

yf yarn forward – bring yarn forward between needles and over right needle to make a st

yo (yon) yarn over needle – take yarn over right needle to make a st

yrn yarn round needle – wrap yarn around right needle from front to back and bring it to front again between needles to make a st

* repeat instructions after asterisk or between asterisks as many times as instructed

[ ] repeat instructions inside [ ]s as many times as instructed

substituting yarns

Knitting patterns always specify a particular brand of yarn. If you decide to use an alternative yarn be sure to calculate the number of balls or hanks you need by the metre (yard) rather than by the yarn weight. If you want to use a different yarn to the one suggested then match the shade as closely as possible.

yarn conversion chart

To convert	multiply by
grams to ounces	0.0352
ounces to grams	28.35
centimetres to inches	0.3937
inches to centimetres	2.54
metres to yards	0.9144
yards to metres	1.0936

UK and US knitting terminology

Most terms used in UK and US knitting patterns are the same, but a few are different. Where terms are different, they appear in the instructions divided by a / .

UK	US
cast off	bind off
moss stitch	seed stitch
stocking stitch	stockinette stitch
tension (size of stitch)	gauge
yarn over needle	yarn over (yo)
yarn forward	yarn over (yo)
yarn round needle	yarn over (yo)

knitting needle conversion chart

This chart shows you how the different knitting needle-size systems compare.

Metric	US sizes	Old UK
2mm	0	14
2¼mm	1	13
2¾mm	2	12
3mm		11
3¼mm	3	10
3¾mm	5	9
4mm	6	8
4½mm	7	7
5mm	8	6
5½mm	9	5
6mm	10	4
6½mm	10½	3
7mm	10½	2
7½mm	11	1
8mm	11	0
9mm	13	00
10mm	15	000

suppliers

Rowan Yarns
Green Lane Mill, Holmfirth
West Yorkshire, HD7 1RW
01484 681881
www.rowanyarns.co.uk

Jaeger Yarns
As Rowan
01484 680050

King Cole Ltd
Merrie Mills, Old Souls Way
Bingley, West Yorkshire
BD16 2AX
01274 561331
www.kingcole.co.uk

Debbie Bliss
Designer Yarns Ltd
Units 8–10
Newbridge Industrial Estate
Pitt Street, Keighley
West Yorkshire
BD21 4PQ
01535 664222
www.debbiebliss.freeserve.co.uk

Personal Threads Boutique
8025 West Dodge Road
Omaha, Nebraska 68114–3413
Phone: (402) 391-7288
Fax: (402) 391-0039
1-800-306-7733 (for orders only)
www.personalthreads.com

index

acknowledgements

author acknowledgements

Thank you to Rosy for her expert pattern checking and for helping me with the writing of this book with Kitty on my knee most of the time! Thank you to CupCake in Brighton for lending me so many beautiful props for the book. Thanks to all at Hamlyn for making the book so stylish and to Rozelle for the beautiful book design and for conveying the essence of my knitwear so well. Last but not least, a big thank you to all the stunning models in this book – you all look so lovely!

publisher acknowledgements

The Publishers would like to thank William Bentley Archer, Charlotte Barton, Olivia Campbell, Daisy Carville, Olivia Dornan, Hannah Goodman, Emily Merrit Moore, Tom Proctor, Ryan Sparham-O'Reilly, Jack Swainston, Kitty Wynne-Mellor, Toby Wynne-Mellor and Mason Young for being such wonderful models. They would also like to thank Jehane Boden Spiers and Zoë Mellor for the kind loan of their homes and Alex Owen for helping with the children throughout the photo shoot.

Executive Editor Sarah Tomley
Managing Editor Clare Churly
Editor Sally Harding
Pattern Checker Rosy Tucker
Executive Art Editor Rozelle Betheim
Designers Maggie Town and Beverly Price
Photographer Adrian Pope
Illustrator Kuo Kang Chen
Production Manager Louise Hall